P9-BJV-666

THE COMPLETE
PATIO
BOOK

By the Editors of Sunset and Southern Living

*Seeded-aggregate paving and supporting structures show off
concrete's versatility (see page 10).*

Unglazed, earth-colored tiles make a handsome, nonskid surface; hand-painted glazed tiles provide accents (see page 23).

Book Editor
Scott Atkinson

Contributing Editor
Fran Feldman

Coordinating Editor
Linda J. Selden

Design
Joe di Chiarro

Illustrations
Bill Oetinger
Rik Olson
Lois Lovejoy

Photographers: Edward Bigelow, 24 top; **California Redwood Association,** 53 bottom; **Glenn Christiansen,** 13 top, 44, 45, 46 bottom; **Derek Fell,** 28; **Richard Fish,** 7; **Philip Harvey,** 4, 11, 31 top, 43 top; **Saxon Holt,** 8, 15, 33 bottom, 54 top, 56 bottom, 57 top, 59; **Jack McDowell,** 16 left, 51; **Stephen Marley,** 24 bottom, 42 right, 48 bottom, 52; **Ells Marugg,** 29 top; **Richard Nicol,** 1, 10, 17, 18, 19 top, 22 bottom, 27 bottom, 32, 34, 56 top, 57 bottom, 60; **Don Normark,** 40; **Norman A. Plate,** 21 bottom, 41, 43 bottom, 48 top, 49 bottom; **Bill Ross,** 9, 16 right, 35, 38 bottom, 39 bottom; **Chad Slattery,** 46 top, 47, 58; **David Stubbs,** 29 bottom; **Rob Super,** 25; **Michael S. Thompson,** 6; **Peter O. Whiteley,** 22 top; **Russ Widstrand,** 13 Bottom, 14 bottom right, 31 bottom; **Tom Wyatt,** 2, 12, 14 top, 14 bottom left, 19 bottom, 20, 21 top, 23, 26, 27 top, 30, 33 top, 36, 38 top, 39 top, 42 left, 50, 53 top, 54 bottom, 55, 80.

A Fresh Look at Patio Living

For many people, the word "patio" simply means a dull concrete rectangle off the back door. But as a glance through the pages of this book will show, today's patio is much more than that. It's actually a total outdoor environment in which attractive paving designs, surrounding structures, amenities, and border plantings all play a part.

This new title is a complete guide to creating the perfect outdoor room. Color photos show you the latest in patio paving styles and amenities, a planning workbook walks you through the design process, and an illustrated, step-by-step how-to chapter outlines building and maintenance instructions.

We are grateful to the following individuals who generously contributed their time and expertise: Richard Casavecchia, Architectural Garden Specialties, Martinez, California; Anne James, Carol R. Johnson & Associates, Cambridge, Massachusetts; F. D. Reinarman, East Greenwich, Rhode Island; and David R. Smith, Concrete Paver Institute, Herndon, Virginia. We also want to thank the following for their help: Architectural Design Products; Dillon Tile Supply, Inc.; Higgins Brick Co.; Import Tile, Co., Inc.; Lyngso Building Materials; Pacific Interlock Pavingstone; Peninsula Building Materials; and Tile Visions.

Special thanks go to Barbara Szerlip for carefully editing the manuscript, to JoAnn Masaoka Van Atta for styling some of the photographs, and to Marianne Lipanovich and Lynne B. Tremble for scouting some of the photography locations.

Cover: Brick stair trim and edgings subtly outline this dining veranda paved with different-size tile. Landscape architect: Robert Chittock. Cover design and photo styling: Susan Bryant. Photography by Richard Nicol.

Editor: Elizabeth L. Hogan

Fourth printing February 1994

Copyright © 1990, Sunset Publishing Corporation, Menlo Park, CA 94025. First edition. World rights reserved. No part of this publication may be reproduced by any mechanical, photographic, or electronic process, or in the form of a phonographic recording, nor may it be stored in a retrieval system, transmitted, or otherwise copied for public or private use without prior written permission from the publisher. Library of Congress Catalog Card Number: 89-69850. ISBN 0-376-01399-0 (SB); ISBN 0-376-09044-8 (SL). Lithographed in the United States.

CONTENTS

SPECIAL FEATURES

TODAY'S OUTDOOR ROOM

I n the past, a patio—better known then as a porch or veranda—served as a vantage point from which the family could quietly admire the garden. Today's patio, however, is much more: a place to engage the great outdoors, relax, entertain friends and family, and actively follow favorite pursuits.

Think of a patio as a bridge between the house and the garden—a transition zone that brings the outdoors into your life. As an extension of your house, a patio can give you all the comforts of indoor living; as part of your garden, it can become a favorite sitting and entertaining area.

There are other benefits, too. Properly planned, a patio can make interior rooms seem more spacious and provide a gracious transition between house and garden. A comfortable outdoor space relieves pressure on indoor entertainment areas. And an attractive patio landscape can enhance your home's value.

Entering a Colorful World

Elegant entry courtyard not only greets guests but also serves as an entertainment area. The uniform tile pattern is bordered by concrete accented with colorful tile inserts. A hedge caps the stuccoed wall, sidestepping code limitations on solid wall height. Architect: Werner & Sullivan. Landscape architect: Robert La Rocca & Associates.

5

Quiet Hideaway
Comfortable seating, a small reflecting pool, wraparound greenery, and a good novel: a small detached patio like this one is a great place to get away from it all.

On the following pages is an overview, in words and photos, of your many options in patio sites, styles, and materials, plus some other basic "building blocks"—edgings, retaining walls, raised beds, pathways, and steps.

Successful Patio Design

Regardless of the size of your lot and any landscaping problems your property may present, successful patio design revolves around several key elements: flexibility, privacy, comfort, safety, and beauty.

■ *Flexibility.* Your design needs to accommodate your family's varying activities, from relaxation and casual gatherings to more active pursuits, such as children's games, barbecues, and entertaining.

■ *Privacy.* As an extension of your indoor living space, your patio should offer the same feeling of privacy as interior rooms do, but with no sense of confinement.

■ *Comfort.* You'll be most comfortable on a patio designed to accommodate your area's climate and your property's microclimate.

■ *Safety.* Patio paving materials have different properties. For example, some become slippery when wet; others are too sharp or uneven for children's games. Traffic patterns from house to patio and from patio to garden need to be safe; also, adequate

lighting should be provided at steps and along garden paths.

■ *Beauty.* Successful patios achieve a certain balance in an overall garden scheme. Materials used in patio construction should blend with those used in the house; colors and textures should harmonize with outdoor landscaping and decorative accents.

Finding the Right Site

Many people think of a patio as a simple rectangle off the back door. If you have a small, flat lot, perhaps that is your best design option. But why not consider a series of interrelated patios connected by steps, or a detached, protected patio in the corner of your lot? Perhaps you can accommodate a secluded patio in a neglected side yard.

A number of options are discussed below (also see the drawing on page 62). Other factors to consider when planning your patio are explained in the chapter beginning on page 61.

Basic backyard patios. The standard backyard rectangle doesn't have to be boring. Edgings, raised

Bold & Modern
This entertainment area's massive trellis rests on stucco columns; low-voltage lights are molded into the uprights. Spaced a tile and a half from the house, the narrow planting strip holds succulents. Design: Suzanne and Rudy Svrcek.

beds, and maybe a gentle curve or two can customize and soften your design. Container or hanging plants and other amenities (see pages 37–59) can also help transform your space.

L- and U-shaped spaces. Houses in the shape of an L or a U offer prime sites for a patio. Surrounding house walls create a ready-made sense of enclosure; privacy screens or an overhead formalize the design. These patios are usually accessible from several rooms at once.

Wraparounds. A flat lot is a natural candidate for a wraparound patio, which allows access from any room along its course while enlarging the apparent size of your house. It may also help you utilize a wasted side yard.

Detached patios. Perfect for creating a quiet retreat, a detached patio works on both flat and sloping lots and is well suited to casual cottage-garden landscapes. Access such a patio by a direct walkway or meandering garden path. Patio roofs, privacy screens, and a tiny fountain are typical additions.

Multilevel patios. Large lots, or those with changes in level, can often accommodate striking multilevel patios, joined by steps or perhaps pathways. Such a layout is usually the best solution when you need multiple use areas.

Balcony Garden

When there's no obvious space for a patio, try looking up: this second-story balcony with built-in bench offers one solution. Planting "beds" house a steadily rotating display of potted flowers.

Rooftop and balcony patios. No open space in the yard? Look up. A garage rooftop adjacent to a second-story living area might be ideal. Or consider a small balcony patio with built-in bench and container plants. Be sure your existing structure can take the extra weight of the wood or masonry (consult an architect or structural engineer). Slope the decking or paving slightly to allow for efficient drainage.

Swimming pool surrounds. When the focus of patio living is a swimming pool, the setting can be formal and rectangular or naturalistic, with the pool blending into an informal landscape. Surround the pool with skidproof masonry and/or low-level wood decking. A patio roof, dining and kitchen area, and spa are effective additions.

Entry patios. Paving, plantings, and perhaps a trickling fountain enclosed by a privacy wall can transform a boring entry path or thirsty front lawn into a private oasis. If local codes prohibit high solid walls, substitute hedges, arbors, or a trellis to let in air and light while blocking street sights and sounds.

Side-yard patios. A neglected side yard may be just the spot for a private, screened sitting area, which can brighten a small, dark bedroom or bath. If you're subject to local fence height restrictions, use arbors or overheads for privacy.

Dinner with a View

Flagstone patio, wrapped in spring finery, makes an elegant spot for outdoor dining. The sloped lot is a natural for this multilevel, detached design. Landscape architect: Katzmaier Newell Kehr.

Industrial Style
Round concrete columns support an angular patio roof that echoes the shape of the patio. The paving and steps are seeded-aggregate (pea-gravel) concrete with steel dividers. A poured concrete retaining wall and raised bed complete the picture. Landscape architect: R. David Adams Associates, Inc.

Sun rooms. Today's sun rooms, which create, in effect, an indoor-outdoor room, are a patio option in harsh climates. Some sun rooms can be opened up when the sun shines and battened down when winter winds howl.

Interior courtyards. If you're designing a new home, consider the most private of patios: an interior courtyard, or atrium. If you're remodeling, perhaps your new living space could enclose an existing patio area.

Patio-deck combinations. Increasingly, homeowners are discovering that patios and decks complement each other. The blend of masonry patios and low-level wood decking allows great flexibility in shape, texture, and finished height. Although masonry surfaces must rest on solid ground, decks tame sloping, bumpy, or poorly draining lots.

Reclaimed driveways. You may have a masonry "patio" already, in the form of an existing driveway. Sometimes, a driveway can do double duty as a patio. Concrete turf blocks soften a driveway's appearance, yet allow for car traffic; planted areas between flagstones or pavers achieve the same effect. Enclosed by a gate and accented with plantings, the area becomes an entry courtyard.

Existing slabs. If you have an old slab, you can either demolish it and start over, or put a new surface on top. Asphalt is best removed in most cases, but an existing concrete slab, unless heavily damaged, can serve admirably as a base for brick, pavers, tile, or stone; or you can top-dress it with colored or stamped concrete. Another possibility is to construct a low-level deck over the slab.

Setting a Style

The first decision you must make is whether you want a formal or informal patio environment.

Formal landscapes are symmetrical, with straight lines, geometric patterns, and perfect balance; they often include sheared hedges, topiaries, and a fountain, pool, or sculpture.

Small, rectangular plots are well suited to the formality of the medieval-knot garden style, with pathways and formal planting beds radiating from a central fountain or sculpture. By replacing the brick or stone with adobe and tile, the style becomes Spanish.

Poured concrete lends a more industrial look to a formal garden. Seeded-aggregate, smooth-troweled, or textured concrete are more modern in feel.

Informal styles, on the other hand, tend toward curves, asymmetry, and apparent randomness; such patios are often lower maintenance. Adjacent plantings are usually more informal, too.

Contemporary designs might feature multilevel surfaces, planters, overheads, a swimming pool, and low-maintenance plantings. Irregular flagstones or mossy bricks laid in sand offer a softer cottage-garden look, as do spaced concrete pavers, especially if you plant ground cover between the units.

Raked gravel that imitates swirling water, carefully placed boulders, a spill fountain, and a hidden garden bench or bridge are all trademarks of a Japanese garden.

In desert climates, the patio can function as a retreat from heat and noise; overheads and screens, a fountain or waterfall, and lush plants with drip lines or spray emitters keep the air cool and moist.

A Perfect Partnership

Mortared brick patio and edging around the swimming pool and spa give way to sleek cedar decking along one side. The combination of masonry paving and wood decking not only looks great but also allows for a smooth change in level. Landscape architect: Royston, Hanamoto, Alley & Abey.

Cottage-garden Retreat

Mossy brick-in-sand paving, a shady trellis, and lacy container plants all add up to a casual, country-garden style. The fireplace at the rear takes the edge off chilly days and evenings. Landscape designer: Josephine Zeitlin.

Brick: Warm & Traditional

Brick is probably the most adaptable and frequently used patio surfacing material available. Set on sand or in mortar, brick provides a handsome, nonglare surface that blends with nearly any architectural style and looks at ease in almost any setting.

Bricks are available in varied colors, sizes, and finishes. Lay them in one of the many basic patterns (for examples, see pages 90–91) or combine several patterns to create striking variations.

Brick does have disadvantages, however. Cost per square foot runs higher than most alternative materials, and, if you lay brick on sand, you may need to give periodic attention to weeds pushing through the joints. A brick surface can be jarringly uneven if the bricks are haphazardly installed. Also, bricks in moist, heavily shaded garden areas can become slick with algaelike growth.

Bricks on Display

Standard brick options include rough common bricks in a variety of colors, smoother face bricks for accents and edgings, bullnose types for stair treads and cap walls, and used and imitation-used styles. Half-thickness paver bricks work well for patios. Precut bricks, shown at bottom, help do-it-yourselfers tackle sophisticated patterns.

Brick types. Although the basic form and composition of brick have remained unchanged for almost 5,000 years, today's builder can choose from thousands of different combinations of colors, textures, and shapes. Of the bewildering variety turned out by brickyards, two basic kinds are used for garden paving: rough-textured common brick and slick face brick.

Most garden paving is done with common brick. People like its familiar color and texture, and it has the undoubted advantage of being less expensive than face brick. Common bricks are more porous than face bricks and less uniform in size and color (they may vary as much as ¼ inch in length).

Most brickyards carry three types of common brick. *Wire-cut brick* is square cut and has a rough texture with little pit marks on its face; lay it to expose the edge if you want a smooth surface. *Sand-mold brick* is slightly larger on one side because it must be turned out of a mold; it's smooth textured and easy to keep clean. *Clinker brick* is noted for its "flashed" patches and surface irregularities caused by overburning; it gives a rough cobblestone effect.

Face brick is not as widely available as common brick; you'll notice it used more frequently for facing walls and buildings than for residential paving. Face brick does make very attractive accents, edgings, header courses, stair nosings, and raised beds—use it anywhere its smooth surface won't present a safety hazard.

Used brick, which may be common or face, has uneven surfaces and streaks of old mortar that can make an attractive informal pavement. Taken from old buildings and walls, these bricks are usually in short supply. Many manufacturers are now converting new bricks to used bricks by chipping them and splashing them with mortar and paint. Manufactured used bricks cost about the same as the genuine article and are easier to find; they're also more consistent in quality than most older bricks.

Low-density firebrick, blonde colored and porous, provides interesting accents, but doesn't wear well as general paving.

Precut brick, another option, is a boon for the do-it-yourselfer venturing out into more complicated bricklaying patterns. Tacks, quoins, bats, sinkers, traps, and spikes are just some of the names for these special shapes, long the domain of a few skilled masons. Expect to pay about the same per unit as for a full-size brick.

All outdoor bricks are graded by their ability to withstand weathering; if you live where it freezes and thaws, buy only those graded SW (severe weathering).

Brick sizes. Most brick is made in modular sizes—that is, the length and width are simple divisions or multiples of each other. This simplifies planning,

Brick Tapestry

Casual brick highlights this patio area, designed to be viewed from the upper stories of the house. Set on a sand base, the bricks, recycled from kiln linings, were positioned and repositioned to get the final composition. Design: John Matthias and Robert Blitzer.

Brick Corridor

Colorful mortared brick pathway leads the eye to the tiled wall fountain in the background. A combination of square bricks in the field, rectangular bricks used as dividers and edgings, and custom-cut detailing creates the subtle design. Landscape architect: Mark Scott Associates.

ordering, and fitting. The standard modular brick measures 8 inches long by 4 inches wide by 2⅔ inches high. Other modular sizes may be available at larger brickyards, in sizes ranging from 12 by 4 by 2 inches to 12 by 8 by 4 inches. Note that all these dimensions are nominal—they include the width of a standard ½-inch mortar joint, so the actual dimensions of the brick are reduced accordingly.

It's common for brick to vary somewhat from specified dimensions. To calculate the quantities of brick you'll need for your project, always visit your building supplier first, with ruler in hand.

Today, you can find many units larger or smaller than the standard dimensions that are excellent for paving. Such bricks belong to the "paver" variety and are roughly half the thickness of standard bricks. "True" or "mortarless" pavers are a standard 4 by 8 inches (plus or minus ⅛ inch) and are a big help when you're laying a complex brick pattern with closed (tightly butted) joints.

Patio in Plaid

This courtyard's brick surface incorporates whole and half sizes and three brick colors; the field is set off by doubled divider courses. Landscape contractor: Richard Casavecchia/Architectural Garden Specialties.

Renaissance Replica

This colorful peacock pattern, accented by red pavers and concrete edgings, lends visual punch to a small backyard. The pattern requires skilled cutting, unless you can find an outlet for precut bricks. Landscape contractor: Richard Casavecchia/Architectural Garden Specialties.

Poolside Surround

Grey mortared brick laid in a 45° herringbone pattern is outlined with vanilla-colored concrete dividers in this formal design. Landscape architect: Mark Scott Associates.

Bird's-eye View

Curved patio of used brick flows through this small backyard space; drought-tolerant plants and stone edgings add to the quiet mood. Landscape designer: Konrad Gauder/Landsculpture.

Concrete: Economical & Versatile

When it comes to pavings around the house, it would be difficult to find a more adaptable material than poured concrete. A mixture of sand, cement, gravel, and water, concrete is even more variable in appearance than brick. Using the proper forms, it can conform to almost any shape. It can be lightly smoothed or heavily brushed, surfaced with handsome pebbles, swirled, scored, tinted, painted, patterned, or cast into molds to resemble other paving materials. And if you get tired of the concrete surface later on, it provides an excellent foundation for brick, stone, or tile set in mortar.

Concrete does have some disadvantages. In some situations, it can be a harsh, hot, and glaring surface. If smoothly troweled, concrete can be slick when wet.

For the do-it-yourselfer, concrete presents additional problems. It must be mixed carefully to exact specifications; there's little room for error. Once the ingredients are combined and water added, you have to work fast; a mistake will require an extensive and, perhaps, costly redo. If the concrete isn't cured correctly or if drainage needs are ignored, the surface may buckle and crack. Site preparation (grading the soil and building wood forms for the pour) can be time-consuming, but the actual pouring and finishing go quickly.

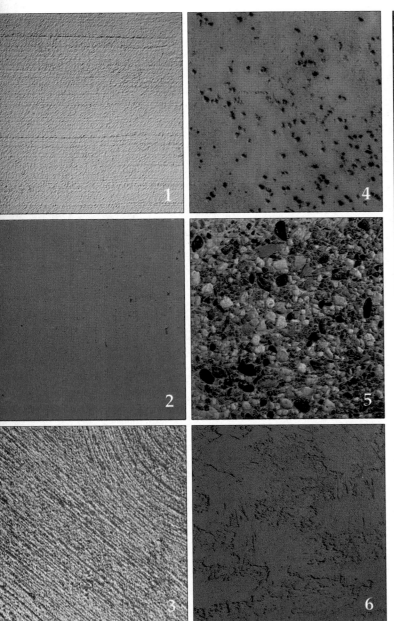

Freeform Pads

Shapes resembling giant stepping-stones are dug into the soil and then filled with concrete. Plantings between pads soften the overall look. Landscape architect: Katzmaier Newell Kehr.

A Look at Concrete Finishes

Shown at left are six basic concrete finishes. Semi-smooth texture (1) is achieved with a wooden float; slick troweled surface (2) is suitable for covered patios; broomed surface (3) is best where maximum traction is needed. Rock salt (4), seeded aggregate (5), and travertine (6) are three popular decorative finishes.

Classic Aggregate

Seeded aggregate, the most popular concrete finish, creates a clean, textured, nonskid surface. An octagonal brick motif borders this eating area, setting it off from the rest of the patio; matching brickwork continues across the landscape. Architect: Curtis Gelotte Architects.

Subtle Stain
Who would guess that this paving is simply poured concrete? The surface was first broom-finished, then acid-washed, and finally stained and sealed. Landscape architect: R. David Adams Associates, Inc.

The trick with concrete is to start small. Plan to divide your work into stages that you and one or two other people can handle. Pour large areas in sections or cast a few paving blocks at a time—this way you can compensate for the large work crew and specialized equipment the contractor has on hand. If you're not sure you want to tackle the job yourself, you may be able to prepare the site and then let professionals take over.

Surface treatments. Concrete pavings are typically given some type of surface treatment, both for appearance's sake and for traction.

Early modern architects often took a "warts and all" approach to concrete texture, reveling in the raw look left by rough surface finishing and construction forms.

You can also wash or sandblast a concrete paving to expose the aggregate, or embed colorful pebbles and stones in it. The second technique, generally known as the seeded-aggregate finish, is probably the single most popular contemporary paving surface. Larger river rocks and fieldstones can also dress up a dull slab.

Other ways to modify the standard steel-troweled concrete surface include color-dusting, staining, masking, sandblasting, acid-washing, and salt-finishing. You or a professional can also stamp and tint concrete to resemble stone, tile, or brick. The patterns simulate either butted joints or open ones, which can then be grouted to look like unit masonry. And other specialty concrete finishes are being developed every year.

Blending concrete with other materials. Uninterrupted expanses of concrete can have a cold, forbidding appearance, unsuited for casual, more informal patio landscape designs. To create visual interest, concrete can be blended with another paving material. Those designs also serve structural purposes, such as adding control joints that help prevent cracking.

Blending concrete and brick is popular; tile and flagstone are other materials that complement concrete. Wood, steel, or copper dividers can act as control joints, as well as allowing the do-it-yourselfer to divide the job up into smaller, more manageable pours.

Stone & Boulder

It might look like stone, but this entry courtyard is actually poured concrete with a stamped, colored topcoat. The dark retaining wall wraps around a boulder, which enhances the native look. Landscape architect: Lankford Associates.

Creating a softer look. Fortunately, there are several techniques that allow concrete to be used in a more casual cottage-garden environment. The surface treatments discussed earlier are a good start: coloring, texturing, and/or stamping make concrete look more natural.

Another softening technique is to lay irregularly shaped chunks of broken concrete in a staggered pattern, with spaces between for planting ground cover. The broken edges and relatively consistent thickness of the concrete give the appearance of sedimentary stone.

You can also simply leave plant pockets in a freshly poured slab, filling them with soil and plants. Drip tubing can be routed to these pockets, allowing plants to be watered thoroughly without soaking the surrounding paving.

Another option for a casual look to concrete is to dig holes or shape curved forms to your own specifications and fill them with concrete. The resulting pads—with plant spaces in between—can be smoothed, textured, and finished to resemble natural stone or seeded with aggregate or another texture just like a standard concrete slab.

Cool Underfoot

Poolside paving is light-colored concrete, with a stripe of Saltillo pavers. The concrete is specially designed for pool surrounds. Landscape architect: Ransohoff, Blanchfield, Jones, Inc.

A Parade of Concrete Pavers

Tough precast concrete pavers come in many shapes, sizes, and colors: common "stepping-stone" pavers, popular "brick" patterns, and numerous cobblestone and interlocking types.

Easy-to-install Concrete Pavers

Concrete pavers, in their dozens of clever shapes, have long been used abroad for everything from patios to roadways. Now made in this country, pavers are being used increasingly in residential work. Precast concrete pavers are an ideal do-it-yourself material. A weekend or two of work laying the pavers—a relatively inexpensive project—can result in a dramatic patio or garden walkway.

Available today in many sizes, colors, and textures, pavers are no longer limited to the familiar 12-inch squares you've seen for years. Shapes include circles, rectangles, and puzzle-piece contours that interlock.

Individual shapes can give way to larger patterns. A simple square can be part of a grid or even a gentle arc. Pavers can butt together to create broad, unbroken surfaces, or they can be spaced apart and surrounded with grass, ground cover, or gravel for interesting textural effect.

Interlocking pavers are a logical industrial descendant of the old-fashioned, labor-intensive cobblestone. Made of extremely dense concrete pressure-formed in special machines and laid in sand with closed (butted) joints, they form a surface more rigid than bricks. No paver can tip out of alignment without taking several of its neighbors with it; thus, the surface remains intact, even under very substantial loads.

Home Turf

Concrete turf blocks and used-brick dividers lend distinction to this motor-court entry (two inconspicuous garages accommodate three cars). It's a green alternative to what might have been a dull expanse of paving. Architect: Bert W. Tarayao. Landscape architect: Richard E. Harrington.

More Paver Styles

Interlocking patterns, like the two designs shown at left, fit together like puzzle pieces. Custom-made adobe, stone, and Saltillo paver replicas (at center) are highly durable. Hollow turf block and small square cobblestone (at right) offer even more variety.

Interlocking pavers are available in tan, brown, red, and natural gray, plus blends of these colors. Modern "cobblestone" patterns are very popular for casual gardens; butt them tightly together and then sweep sand or soil between the irregular edges.

Turf blocks, a special paver variant, are designed to carry light traffic while retaining and protecting ground cover plants. These allow for the possibility of grassy patios and driveways, as well as side-yard access routes that stand up to wear.

Concrete "bricks," available in classic red as well as imitation "used" or antique, are increasingly popular substitutes for the real thing; in many areas, they're significantly less expensive.

Different-size circles, squares, and rectangles can be found at most building and garden supply centers. Availability may vary depending on location. Cost is determined by size and texture; for example, a 12-inch square of 1½-inch-thick concrete seeded with pebbles can cost three times as much as a plain or colored paver of the same size.

Some landscape professionals cast their own pavers in custom shapes, textures, and colors: adobe, stone, and tile replicas are just a few of the options. You can also make your own pavers, though they won't be as strong as standard pressure-formed units.

A word of caution: Be careful when choosing colored concrete pavers; sometimes, the pigment is very shallow, and bare concrete may show through deep scratches and chips.

Like Hand-cut Stone

These pavers, with their beveled edges and different colors and shapes, combine in several geometric patterns. Design: Patternstone.

Gray & Green
This muted checkerboard surface was a labor of love: the homeowners prepainted each square with custom-mixed tennis court paint. Design: Irene and Barry Grenier.

All in a Whorl
To capitalize on an upstairs view, cobblestone pavers were painstaking laid in a whorled pattern. Landscape architect: Joan A. Lankford.

Ceramic Tile: Rustic to Elegant

Tile works well in both formal and informal garden situations. The warm, earthy browns and reds of ceramic tile blend with natural outdoor colors, and the hand-fired pigments are permanent and nonfading.

Smoother than almost any other garden paving surface, tiles are easy to clean and wax. For this reason, they're particularly well suited to areas subject to soiling, such as outdoor cooking areas. Because tile looks as great indoors as out, it's a good material to use on the surface of both an indoor room and the patio or outdoor room that's an extension of it.

Tile paving does have some drawbacks that should be considered, however. It's quite costly compared with brick—twice to three times as much per square foot. Because tiles are so hard, they're difficult to shape. Also, the smooth, slick surface of some kinds of tile, especially when waxed, can give off harsh reflections and provide little traction when wet, a disadvantage around a swimming pool or built-in spa.

To prolong the life of tiles, it's best to install them over concrete or wood decking, even though this involves additional time and expense.

Glazed or unglazed? Glaze is a hard finish, usually including a color, applied to the surface of the clay body before final baking. Most of the bright, flashy tiles you see in tile display rooms are glazed.

But unless a special grit has been added to the glazed tiles, they may be slippery when wet. The solution? Opt for unglazed outdoor tiles, saving the colorful glazed tiles for occasional accents or for edgings and raised planting beds.

Tile types. Most outdoor tile falls into one of four groups: patio tile, quarry tile, pavers, or synthetic stone.

■ *Patio tile*, which comes in red, tan, yellow, and brown, is fairly irregular in shape. Because these tiles absorb water easily, they may crack if frozen.

■ *Quarry tile* is more expensive and more regular in shape than patio tile. It comes glazed or unglazed in natural clay colors of yellow, brown, or red. Outdoor tiles have a rougher surface than the glazed kinds normally used indoors. They're available with rounded edges and in corrugated finishes.

■ *Pavers*, like quarry tiles, are molded rather than extruded before they're fired. Available in numerous colors, shapes, and sizes, pavers are generally unglazed and are usually sealed to make them water-resistant.

■ *Synthetic stone* is now being developed by tile manufacturers spurred by the increasing popularity

Closeup on Tiles

From earthy to brightly colored and from rough to slick, tiles are great both for accent and as expanses of paving. Unglazed terra-cotta and presealed Saltillo pavers are across the top; at top right is slate cut to tile size. The beige square with individual "pickets" forms an octagon; man-made stone tiles are at lower right. Colorful hand-painted tiles from Mexico (left) and Tunisia (right) work well as accents—they're too slick for overall paving.

Careful Organization

Large tile pavers march evenly over this welcoming courtyard, which serves as a private patio as well. Landscape architect: Ransohoff, Blanchfield, Jones, Inc.

Inside Out
A truly versatile flooring, these low-fired Mexican pavers are equally at home indoors and out on the patio. Pointed pickets add pattern variety. Inside, the pavers are coated with masonry sealer; outdoors, they're left bare. Architect: Edward Giddings.

Earthy Elegance
Terra-cotta tile gives this dining room patio a sophisticated informality. The units were laid over a concrete slab; matching tiles, in a larger size, cover the adjoining concrete seat wall. Architect: John E. MacAllister.

Heading Southwest

Adobe's natural, warm color contrasts with a splashy display of multicolored impatiens. The winding path was laid in a basket weave pattern with butted joints. The blocks, cut with a hand saw, rest on a bed of crushed rock.

of stone. These tiles, which mimic the look of granite and sandstone, generally have enough surface bite to be used on patios. Colors include black and various shades of gray and beige, with patterns of varying intensity. Sizes vary from 3 to 12 inches square.

Adobe for Regional Character

Few paving materials can add a rustic, friendly tone to an informal garden living area the way adobe does. Spaced with 1-inch open joints, adobe provides an excellent base for a living floor; low-growing plants and moss fill the joints, softening the look of the surface.

Historically, adobe structures were doomed to decay, eventual victims of the annual duel between summer heat and winter rain. Today's adobe, however, is made with an asphalt stabilizer that keeps the bricks from dissolving.

Although found almost exclusively in Arizona, New Mexico, and Southern California, adobe can be used effectively almost anywhere in the country. However, delivery charges outside the West can make it an uneconomical paving choice.

All adobe blocks commonly used in construction are made by the same process and have nearly the same textural quality. They're generally 4 inches thick by 16 inches long, with widths varying from 3½ to 12 inches. The most common block is 4 by 7½ by 16 inches, about the same as four or five clay bricks put together. Blocks can range in weight from 12 to 45 pounds.

In addition, a nonstandard block has been designed specifically for paving use. Available in face sizes of 12 by 12 inches or 6 by 12 inches with a 2½-inch depth, this block contains more asphalt than can be used for blocks in walls.

Because the blocks are large, adobe construction proceeds quickly, and your efforts yield immediate results.

Stone: An Old Standby

Stone pavings offer the warmth of a thoroughly natural material, and most are very durable. Flat flagstones and cut stone tiles are ideal for formal paving. For a more informal look, you can use more irregularly shaped rocks and pebbles, setting them on soil or embedding them in concrete.

Marble and granite are examples of igneous, or magna-formed, rocks; these are usually the toughest choices. Earth-toned sandstone, limestone, and other sedimentary stones are more porous; they usually have a chalky or gritty texture. Dense, smooth slate is a fine-grained metamorphic rock.

The availability of stone types, shapes, sizes, and colors depends on locale; price usually increases with distance from the quarry. Generally, stone pavings are expensive and the surface may be slippery when wet.

Flagstone. Technically, flagstone is any flat stone that's either naturally thin or split from rock that cleaves easily. Flagstone works in almost any garden setting; its natural, unfinished look blends well with plants, and it's one of the few paving materials that can be placed directly on stable soil. Its subdued colors—buff, yellow, brownish red, and gray—add warmth to a patio, and its irregularly shaped slabs contribute texture.

Flagstone does have some less favorable attributes. It's very costly (five to ten times as much as brick or concrete) and it's not a good surface for outdoor furniture, games, or wheeled playthings because of its irregularity. Also, some types of stone

Swirling Flagstone

Viewed from above, this irregular flagstone patio seems to whirl and wave; the earth-tone mortar provides contrast. Brick divider courses and edgings accentuate the fluid shape. Design: Matthew Yrigoyen/Full Circle Earth Works.

soil easily and are difficult to clean (ask your supplier about the characteristics of the flagstone you're considering). Flagstones must be laid out very carefully to avoid ending up with an awkward-looking patchwork design.

Flagstones generally range in thickness from ½ inch to 2 inches.

Stone tiles. Many stone types are available precut to rectangular shapes. You can also find hand-cut squares and rectangles in random sizes. Slate, avail-

A Stone Sampler

This selection of stone types is only a sampling of what's available; you'll probably discover more in your area. At top left are regularly cut stone "tiles"; below is irregular sandstone in several different shades. A piece of angular cobblestone is at top right; below are a pair of fieldstones suitable for paving. At bottom right is a collection of smooth river rocks that can be used for mosaics.

Casually Formal

Formal dark flagstone is carefully cut and laid in whorls, broken up with areas of crazy paving—smaller fieldstones surrounded by informal plantings. The retaining wall repeats the shapes and color of the crazy paving. Landscape designer: Four Dimensions.

Open to View

This slate comes in rectangles of varied dimensions and depths; the units are laid out carefully with very narrow joints, then mortared for elegant results. The bordering wall provides contrasting texture. Landscape architect: Robert Chittock.

A Cobbled Corner

A traditional cobblestone paving lends a comfortable feel to this detached garden patio. The stones must be laid in firm soil or sand; soil and plantings fill the spaces between the units.

able in many colors, and granite are both popular choices, though they are expensive.

Other stones. Fieldstones, river rocks, and pebbles offer alternatives to the high cost of flagstone. These water-worn or glacier-ground stones produce rustic, uneven pavings that make up for in charm what they may lack in smoothness underfoot.

River rocks and pebbles are widely available in countless shapes and sizes, are impervious to weather, and are virtually maintenance-free. Smaller stones and pebbles can be set or seeded in concrete; large stones can be laid directly on soil as raised stepping-stones. An entire surface can be paved solid with cobblestones set in concrete or tamped earth.

For small areas, you can make intricate patterns of pebble mosaic. Narrow mosaic panels are very effective for breaking up an expanse of concrete or brick.

There are some negatives to consider. Natural stones are very smooth and can be slippery, especially in wet weather. Because their shapes are irregular, they may be uncomfortable to walk on; this is especially true of rounded cobblestones.

After the Rain

This formal slate paving glistens after a summer shower, blending in softly with its surroundings. Rectangular units are repeated on the steps and retaining walls.

Laying the surface, particularly when you're working with small pebbles and stones in mortar or concrete, is a very slow process. It's best to confine this surfacing to a limited area.

The Warmth of Wood

With its pleasing color and texture, wood paving—whether rounds, blocks, or railroad ties— brings something of the forest into the garden. When you add soil and plantings around the units, you enhance the natural informality of wood even more.

Other good uses for wood outdoors include a low-level wood deck, perfect for bridging uneven spots or extending a flat patio past a grade falloff, and wood pathways and steps. Because wood blends well with other paving materials, it can be used easily in transition zones between masonry patio areas.

Wood rounds, blocks, and ties. Wood may be used as paving in several ways: round disks can be embedded in random patterns in sand over gravel, square blocks can be laid like brick, or railroad ties can be combined with other paving materials or ground covers for a bold-looking, durable surface.

Rounds and blocks of redwood, cedar, or cypress will eventually have to be replaced, because the end grain is constantly in contact with ground moisture that seeps up through the sand or gravel bed; treating the wood with a preservative before installation helps. These surfaces are sensitive to weather, too: they can crack and warp in sunny locations, or freeze and split in heavy frosts.

Railroad ties, pretreated against rot and insect damage, will endure the elements for many years. Standard ties measure 6 by 8 inches by 8 feet long and weigh anywhere from 100 to 140 pounds each. (In some areas, 2½-foot lengths are also available.)

Low-level decks. Wood used for decking is durable and resilient underfoot, and does not store heat the way other surfacing materials can. In addition, its light weight (2 to 12 pounds per square foot) makes installation very convenient for the novice do-it-yourselfer. And because it's available in a wide variety of species, grades, and sizes, wood adapts easily to individual budgets and architectural styles. Depending on the effect you desire, you can let the deck weather naturally, or you can paint, stain, oil, or bleach it.

Wood decks do need periodic maintenance. You may need to remove mildew or fungus, rust stains from nails, and splinters; or the finish may require a touchup. Unlike other outdoor surfacing materials, wood is vulnerable to fire and termites.

Changing Level
Built over an existing patio, this handsome deck provides a center for alfresco meals and relaxation. The wood picnic table and benches match the deck; the hot tub is transformed into a table when its wooden lid is in place. Design: Ed Hoiland.

Up on the Roof
This garage-top eating area, accessed from the second-story dining room, captures both the sun and the view. The roof structure was beefed up and pitched for drainage. Architect: Robert Swatt and Bernard Stein.

Loose Materials

For economy, good drainage, and a more casual look, consider including such loose materials as gravel, redrock, or wood chips in your patio plan. Think of these as "filler" materials to both accent and stretch your patio borders.

Gravel can be raked into patterns or set into decorative openings in other paving materials; or you can separate different gravel types with dividers. Gravel or wood chips can be combined with concrete pads, concrete pavers, or other stepping-stones. Loose materials also complement plants in transition zones between the patio and garden.

Unless compacted, loose materials are easily scattered and difficult to walk on. They also tend to be pestered by weeds growing through them. (You can avoid this problem by laying the materials over a sheet of heavy plastic or filter fabric.) They stand up best when they cover a more permanent bed of pea gravel or decomposed granite.

Wood chips and bark. By-products of lumber mills, wood chips and bark are springy and soft underfoot, generally inexpensive, and easy to apply. To work successfully as a patio surface, they should be confined inside a grid with headers.

Wood chips make a good cushion under swings and slides in children's play areas. Sometimes called gorilla hair, shredded bark is the most casual of these loose materials; it compacts well and is useful as a transitional material between plantings.

Gravel. Gravel is collected or mined from natural deposits. Crushed rock has been mechanically fractured and then graded to a uniform size. If the surface of the rock has been naturally worn smooth by water, it's called river rock. Frequently, gravels are named after the regions where they were quarried.

When making a choice, consider color, sheen, texture, and size. Take home samples as you would paint chips. Keep in mind that gravel color, like paint color, becomes more intense over a large area.

Crushed rock compacts firmly for stable footing on paths and walkways, but its sharp edges may hurt bare feet. Smooth river rock feels better, but tends to roll underfoot. Small river rock, also called pea gravel, is easiest to rake.

Redrock. Available under different names depending on location, redrock is a reddish, rocky clay that compacts when dampened and rolled. Along with decomposed granite, which is similar but longer lasting and more expensive, redrock can be put down alone or used as a foundation for another paving material. In time, the redrock surface will wear away, dissolving into dust.

Bags of Plenty
Loose paving materials are available by the sack or by the truckload. Shown, from top to bottom, are "gorilla hair" (shredded bark), redwood chips, decomposed granite, quartz pebbles, redrock, and river rocks.

Chess, Anyone?

This highly sculptured study in dark pea gravel and vanilla-colored concrete is broken by a poured concrete bench and curb and by planting beds strewn with redwood chips. Landscape architect: Robert La Rocca & Associates.

Rooftop River

Gray blue stones lie in a streamlike path in a bed of tan gravel chips in this small-scale rooftop garden. Landscape architect: Isabelle Greene.

Edgings

Edgings, the borders immediately adjacent to your patio surface, serve three main purposes: they contain both the patio material (especially when units are laid in sand or loose) and the surrounding soil, they serve as a transition between the paving and the surrounding landscaping, and they're a decorative element in their own right.

Most garden edgings are made of wood, but brick or other masonry units, poured concrete, and stone are also used. A patio or terrace composed of masonry units, such as concrete pavers, with dividers spaced every few feet practically requires an edging made of the same material as the dividers to achieve a finished appearance.

Edgings can be used to visually link disparate elements in the landscape. Using brick to edge a

lawn, an exposed-aggregate patio, and a gravel path, for example, will unify the overall design. Edgings can also connect different areas of a garden: a brick-edged patio, for example, may taper off to a brick path that leads to another area, again edged with brick.

Retaining Walls

If your lot has sloping areas, you may need to include a retaining wall in your patio plan. Besides its structural contributions, a retaining wall plays a major esthetic role as well.

Wood, both attractive and easy to work with, is a popular material for a retaining wall. Be sure to use a decay-resistant species or pressure-treated lumber designed for contact with the earth. For low walls, you can lay uncut stones or chunks of broken concrete without mortar or footings. For higher walls, concrete footings and mortared joints are required for stability. Concrete blocks, bricks (for walls no higher than about 2 feet), and adobe are also suitable, especially when reinforced with steel.

Edgings in Gray & Green
Lush grasses form a graceful green border between the concrete paving and a knee wall. The preformed concrete was mixed to stone color, sandblasted, and then sealed. Landscape architect: R. David Adams Associates, Inc.

Stone Picnic Niche

A weighty but charming stone retaining wall blends with the paving, creating the perfect spot for a built-in bench and a wood picnic table. Landscape designer: Philip Neumann.

A Boulder Border

A used-brick header course curves around a natural garden pool. Beyond, edging stones restrain the paving. Landscape designer: Konrad Gauder/ Landsculpture.

Where engineering is critical, poured concrete may be the only solution. Often, you can dress up the wall with a surface veneer.

If your retaining wall is more than 3 feet high, if you have expansive soil, or if you live in a seismic zone, consult your building department for design regulations.

Raised Beds

Raised beds combine decoration and practicality in a single package. They're usually easy to build and, depending on their size, moderate in cost.

On gently sloping hillsides, raised beds can provide level areas for plantings. On a flat lot, they create visual relief and elevate special plantings into positions of prominence. Raised beds that adjoin a house extend its architectural lines into the garden, providing a transition zone where plants can frame and soften the patio and house. When provided

with broad tops at a convenient height, the beds also make comfortable seats.

For the gardener, raised beds offer control over soil composition and drainage, and elevate plants to a convenient working level. Drip irrigation lines are easy to work into a raised bed scheme.

Pathways

Although the shortest distance between two points is, of course, a straight line, garden walks usually work best where this idea is ignored, at least when utility isn't the overriding concern.

Whatever its direction, a walk is most interesting when it provides a series of experiences along the way. For example, it can alternately reveal and conceal special plantings, garden sculpture, or an interesting view. On a small lot, visual space is expanded when you conceal the pathway's end or use "forced perspective," gradually diminishing the width of the path to make it appear longer.

Keep appropriateness uppermost in mind when selecting materials. Major access walks should be made of brick, concrete, unglazed tile, or stone slabs for easy traffic flow and an even, nonskid surface.

Garden Steps

Garden steps can be gracious accents that set the mood for an entire landscaping scheme.

Most inviting are wide, deep steps that lead the eye to a garden focal point; such steps can also serve as a retaining wall, a base for a planter, or additional seating space. To soften the edges of a series of steps, as well as help mark them for walkers, place containers, plantings, or open beds along their borders.

Constructing steps of the same material used in the patio or for garden walls helps unite an overall landscaping plan. Using contrasting materials draws attention to the steps and those areas of the garden they serve. Combining materials can effect a transition between unlike surfaces. For example, you can link a brick patio to a concrete walk with steps made of concrete treads and brick risers.

Regardless of the material you use, put safety first: treads should give safe footing in wet weather, and adequate lighting must be provided.

At the Foot of the Stairs
Spaced, mortared bullnose bricks set off the curved landing, forming a striking transition zone between the stairs and the patio surface. Landscape designer: Walter S. Kerwin/Swanson's Nursery & Landscaping.

Along the Way

This multilevel stone patio moves from the veranda to a detached landing at a lower level; the matching steps and retaining wall tie all the elements together. Landscape architect: Katzmaier Newell Kehr.

Path Meets Patio

The weathered brick pavement in the foreground serves as the patio floor; the footpath leading into the garden is river-washed stone. Landscape architect: Erik Katzmaier and Yana Ruzicka.

THE FINISHING TOUCHES

S tructural elements, such as paving, edgings, and retaining walls, form the
"foundation" of your patio. But when it
comes to comfort, function, and style, it's
the amenities you add that count.

For versatility and interest, it's hard to
beat a patio roof or gazebo. Offering shade
and shelter, it extends the number of hours
you can use your patio at the same time
that it adds an attractive design element. A
simple vertical screen can contribute a
feeling of private space, as well as divide
your patio into use areas. An outdoor room
provides an airy space for relaxing and
entertaining.

Adding a barbecue, or even a complete
outdoor kitchen, efficient outdoor lighting,
and a heating or cooling system makes your
patio more useful, extending the patio
season into the fall and winter months.

Popular for relaxing soaks, spas and hot
tubs can be easily tucked into most patio
designs. For water of a different sort, con-

A Quiet Glow

*An illuminated bridge over the water
leads the eye and lights the way to the
gazebo in the background. The gazebo's
fanciful curves are cut from 2 by 12s;
trim disks and straps are copper. Bridge
lights are submersible pool fixtures
shining through glass blocks embedded in
the bridge. Architect: Mark Hajjar.*

Bold Sun Shelter

Facing the Pacific, this attached overhead with its simple, uncluttered lines throws shade on both the patio and the house until the sun melts into the horizon. Landscape architect: John J. Greenwood & Associates, Inc.

Poolside Pavilion

This freestanding patio roof, more a "space frame" than a true shelter, defines the spa and pool area. Downlights project from the stucco columns, which match the house and walls; sturdy plates anchor the beams. Decorative tail cuts liven up the rafters. Landscape design: G. Grisamore Design, Inc.

sider a garden pool, fountain, or waterfall; each can wrap your patio in coolness and privacy.

Finishing touches that provide both comfort and color include storage units, furniture, and container plants.

Patio Roofs

Properly planned and installed, a patio roof, whether freestanding or attached to your house, can bring welcome shade to an expanse of hot paving and allow you to use your outdoor space even during summer showers. Your patio's exposure to the sun may dictate the kind of overhead protection you'll need; wind is an additional factor.

When you're planning a roof, be sure its color and structural elements will harmonize with your patio, house, and garden.

The basic framework. In most cases, support for a patio overhead comes from a simple frame made of wood posts and beams (for construction details, see pages 98–99). Although wood posts are standard, concrete, steel, and stucco are increasingly used to provide exceptional strength or to blend with the design of the house.

Framing connections, which often determine the overall style of the overhead, can be made most easily with prefabricated metal connectors. Welders can custom-make connectors to create a more finished appearance. Increasingly, overhead structures make use of "sandwich" construction, where pairs of beams or rafters flank the posts they're joined to; the connection is then made with long through-bolts.

Choosing a cover. Your patio roof can be permanent, adjustable, or portable. To permit easy clearance and to avoid a closed-up feeling, make the roof at least 8 feet above the patio surface.

■ *Lath, batten, and lumber.* The most common type of lath is made of rough-surfaced redwood, cedar, or cypress, milled to about ⅜ inch by 1½ inches and sold in lengths of up to 8 feet. Batten resembles overgrown lath and is available in lengths of up to 20 feet. Boards and framing lumber may also be used as lath.

Using preassembled wood lattice (crisscrossed lath) panels lets you avoid the tedious work of measuring, cutting, and fastening lath pieces individually. The panels are manufactured in 4- by 8-foot, 2- by 8-foot, and 4- by 6-foot sizes and in various patterns.

Lath makes a good overhead where you need vertical air circulation but not a watertight cover. But lath casts sharply defined stripes of shadow that

you may find annoying, especially when you're trying to read.

For a permanent, airy, and tailored patio shelter that will block the sun at certain times and let it pour in at others, consider adjustable or fixed louvers.

■ *Reed, bamboo, and other woven woods.* Among the lightest and most appealing overhead cover materials are woven reed, bamboo, spruce, and basswood. Many people prefer their soft, irregular shade patterns to the harsher shadows cast by lath. Under normal conditions, expect them to last for several seasons (bamboo longer than reed).

■ *Outdoor fabrics.* Colorful and water-resistant, canvas and synthetic outdoor fabrics can block or diffuse sun, shed rain, and add color and texture to a home or garden.

Today, synthetic acrylic fabrics have edged canvas out of the top spot. Acrylics, which should last 5 to 10 years, have a soft, woven look and are offered in a broad palette of colors and patterns, though the colors may not be as crisp as those painted on canvas. Translucency varies with color.

■ *Screening materials.* Screening, usually aluminum or fiberglass, filters sunlight and, when fine meshes are used, repels insects and pests. In coastal areas, opt for noncorrosive plastic—either plastic mesh or greenhouse shadecloth.

■ *Plastic and glass.* Plastic and glass provide protection from rain and snow while still allowing plenty of light to penetrate. When used improperly, however, a plastic or glass roof can act as a heat trap or create a condensation and drip problem, making life beneath it miserable.

Acrylic is shatter-resistant, weighs less than glass, and can be transparent or translucent in almost every color or tint in the rainbow. Sheets of acrylic are easy to cut, drill, and fasten. On the negative side, acrylic scratches easily. Remember, also, that any color will shed the same color light on the surfaces beneath it.

Polyester resin and vinyl panels, often reinforced with fiberglass, are widely used patio roofing materials. Translucent types are the most popular.

Glass is occasionally used for an enclosed greenhouse-type space. Consult a design professional if you want to use it.

■ *Solid roofing.* Such solid roofing materials as shingles and tile can be used very effectively, provided the material blends with the one used on your house. A solid roof usually requires one or more layers of underlayment (typically plywood) and, if attached to the house, perhaps some flashing. Be sure the roof is slightly pitched to allow for runoff.

Window Wall

Offering an intriguing glimpse of the garden beyond, a new window breaks up the masonry expanse (as does the new bench) in what was once a solid wall between two patios. Landscape architect: Richard William.

Plant Tapestry

A two-way wall of bright flowers and foliage separates a small patio from the street, enlivening both the street-side view and the patio. The tubular-steel growing frame, 14 inches thick, is wrapped with chain-link fencing; the verticals are anchored in concrete. Sphagnum covers the fencing, with lightweight potting soil filling the frame. Two drip systems on timers accommodate the differing watering needs of each side. Design: Cher and Bob Truskowski.

Gazebos

When you think of a gazebo, do you imagine a classic latticework Victorian summerhouse for entertaining guests or a simple garden retreat where you can relax and watch the setting sun? Either way, it's instant shade for people and plants, a destination within your own garden.

Traditionally speaking, a gazebo is a freestanding version of a patio roof, with six or eight sides and sloping rafters joined in a central hub at the roof peak. Usually, the hexagonal or octagonal sides are partially closed in with lath, lattice, or even metal grillwork.

Gazebo construction can be substantial or quite light, and style can vary from strikingly modern to thoroughly traditional. Built-in perimeter seating and such amenities as sinks, barbecues, and spas lend versatility.

Several companies manufacture gazebos in kit form, complete except for the foundation. Many kits offer choices in railings and other details. Typically, you construct the gazebo on a concrete slab or low-level deck. Assembly usually takes a weekend or two and requires only basic tools and skills.

Screens for Shelter & Privacy

Vertical screens can curtail intrusions by unwanted sun, wind, or noise, as well as by too-near neighbors. Another function of vertical screens is to define space: they can demarcate a patio in the front yard, for example, or separate various use areas in the back. Screens can also camouflage unsightly objects, such as air conditioners.

Many of the materials that work for overheads work for vertical screens. Consider function, style, and strength when you're choosing a material.

Shades and screens. Roll-down shades made of woven reed, bamboo, or basswood (a material similar to bamboo but with a more polished appearance) can often provide the necessary protection from unwanted wind, sun, and noise. So can shades made of outdoor fabric.

Aluminum screening protects against sun as well as against insects and windborne litter. Moreover, screening doesn't block views.

Wood screens and fences. More substantial than roll-down shades or screening are freestanding

Open-air Conservatory

*Lattice encloses a former entry patio to make a room paved
with brick and filled with plants. Openings frame garden views;
the lattice hides a retaining wall. The roof has fiberglass panels
for all-weather protection. Design: Larry Cain.*

Dining Alfresco

*A patio roof, hanging ferns, a low railing, and a plant display
table transform this veranda into an outdoor room perfect for
dining. The curtains can be drawn when shelter is required—
they'll still let filtered light through.*

wood screens and fences. When made of vertical or
latticed lath or sections punctuated with evergreen
shrubs, they provide a measure of privacy (as well
as ventilation) to a garden that doesn't require complete protection.

Where seclusion is important, look to solid
board fencing, grapestakes, translucent plastic panels framed with wood, or basket-weave fencing.
Translucent plastic screens can admit light to a dark
corner without allowing outsiders to see in.

If you want to break up a blank expanse of
wall, a simple oval or square window or cutout, especially when placed to frame a view, lends a sense
of mystery and discovery to a garden. On the practi-

cal side, windows or cutouts can improve air circulation in a confined area. Clear plastic or tempered
glass panels are also particularly effective wind-
breaks where you don't want to obstruct the view.

Although few communities permit fences
higher than 6 feet, you can apply for a variance if
you need to block the view from a neighbor's porch
or second-story window. Remember, too, that tall
fences are difficult to build. One solution is to train
a plant to rise above fence height.

Screening with plants and trees. Vines trained onto
lattice trellises or wire frames can block wind and
sun, yet still give an airy, open feeling to your patio.

Many deciduous vines grow quickly to cover a large area, leafing out in summer as your need for shade increases. (Choose plants that don't attract bees or other insects, and remember that if you choose a rampant grower, such as wisteria or clematis, you'll have to prune frequently.)

Sheared evergreen hedges give a patio a sense of enclosure. Higher hedges, especially dense ones, make excellent insulators against noise.

Trees, of course, are the most striking elements you can use to protect your outdoor space. The right tree in the right location will help break brisk winds, protect your patio from hot summer sun, and add sculptural value of its own. Make your selection carefully: once a tree is planted, it's usually there to stay.

An Outdoor Room

Half-sheltered, half-exposed, an outdoor room is a traditional space that's part garden, part house. It offers some protection from the elements, but its open side walls let garden fragrances and breezes swirl through. With some careful planning of the garden views adjacent to the room, you'll be able to provide an almost seamless transition between indoor and outdoor spaces.

It's hard to define the "typical" outdoor room. It may be a sun room, a detached pavilion, an atrium, or a sheltered interior courtyard. It may consist solely of a shady arbor or have a solid roof and screens. It can house extensive furnishings, a complete kitchen and buffet area, or simply an intimate dining area for two.

Because many have fireplaces and solid roofs, outdoor rooms are useful year-round spaces for alfresco entertaining or relaxation. Where humidity is low and mosquitoes aren't bothersome, these garden-oriented rooms don't need to be glassed or screened in.

But if your climate is not so agreeable, you can use any of the materials discussed for patio roofs, gazebos, and privacy screens and fences to make the room more comfortable. Some outdoor rooms can even be glassed in during the cooler months of the year.

Today's retractable patio roofs open up new possibilities—facilitating a sun bath or meteor shower in clear weather, a secure "indoor" space on stormier days.

In the roof structure, flush-mounted downlights can illuminate the space at night. Uplights accent plants while remaining unobtrusive. Subtle, well-balanced garden lighting further blurs the distinction between indoor and outdoor spaces. See pages 47–49 for details on planning your lighting scheme.

The Movable Roof

This outdoor room knows no off-season, thanks to the large retractable skylight. An existing interior atrium in this home lent itself to this simple "bridging" design. Skylight design: Rollamatic Roofs, Inc.

Southwestern Ramada

A sturdy trellis supported by a formal colonnade creates a sense of enclosure in this ramada. The 35-foot-long corridor has a waist-high fireplace at one end and a large wall fountain in the center. The room steps down 18 inches, turning its tile-clad retaining walls into benches. Landscape architect: Don Bonar.

A Do-it-yourself Experience

As many as eight diners can pull up to this tiled octagonal table, complete with a barbecue in the center. The circular grill, well within reach of all diners, can be raised or lowered over flame-heated lava rocks; a key in the barbecue pedestal turns on the gas.

Barbecues

Barbecues range from classic masonry structures to permanent or portable manufactured units. Whatever style you choose, be sure to plan enough working space (built-in or collapsible) beside the grill for dishes, pans, and barbecue accessories.

Built-in units. Today's sophisticated masonry units are likely to incorporate built-in smokers, commercial woks, and pizza ovens along with the traditional grill. The focal points for outdoor entertaining, these barbecues are big, bold, permanent structures designed for dedicated backyard chefs. Many units include serving counters where guests can enjoy food hot off the grill.

Plan the location of a built-in unit carefully. Ideally, the unit should be both close to the kitchen and sheltered from the weather. Downlighting (see pages 47–49) helps stretch your barbecuing hours.

Most communities have very strict ordinances about outdoor fires. Check with your local fire department and building inspection department before you or your contractor begin work on a permanent unit.

Portable barbecues. Portables are a good choice if you prefer not to confine your cooking to one spot in the garden, if you can't fit a permanent structure into your patio plan, or if you want to be able to move the barbecue under a shelter during inclement weather. The three main types of portables are charcoal fired, gas, and electric.

■ *Charcoal-fired barbecues.* The most popular charcoal-fired barbecues are open braziers, covered kettles, and boxes with hinged lids.

Open braziers are available in various sizes, from table-top portables and hibachis to larger models. Many braziers feature a cooking grill that can be raised or lowered to adjust the distance between firebed and food, thus controlling the heat.

Covered kettles are available in various sizes; the 18- and 24-inch models are the most common. Dampers on the lid and under the firebox allow you to adjust air flow and control the heat. This type of barbecue provides the same even heat as an oven and is ideal for cooking large cuts of meat, whole fish, or whole poultry.

Kettle barbecues may also be used for grilling over direct heat. Leaving the lid off makes it easier to watch and tend quick-cooking foods, but many manufacturers recommend covering the grill to speed up cooking and conserve fuel.

Barbecue boxes with hinged lids function similarly to covered kettles. You can use them covered for cooking by indirect heat, or open or closed for grilling over direct heat. Many have firebeds that can be raised and lowered; spit-roasting attachments are available for some models.

■ *Gas and electric barbecues.* Barbecues powered by gas or electricity provide two alternatives to charcoal-fired barbecues. Models using natural or bottled gas include kettles and single or double box-shaped units; barbecues heated by electric coils are available in a similar range of styles.

Outdoor units fueled by bottled gas usually roll on wheels; natural gas units are mounted on a fixed pedestal and need to be connected to a gas line. Electric units can simply be plugged into the nearest outlet. All gas units and some electric models employ a special briquet-shaped material above the burner. When meat juices drip on these hot "briquets," smoke rises to penetrate and flavor the food.

Chinese-style Smoker Oven

An oven fits in a separate chimney between a large, patio-warming fireplace on the left and a smaller one on the right. A gas jet regulates the oven to allow brined salmon to smoke slowly at low heat (160° to 180°) or to permit duck or Chinese-style pork to roast at higher temperatures. Landscape architect: Thomas L. Berger Associates.

From Smoker to Wok

Two-chamber smoker has a fire-building compartment at the bottom, racks for hanging fish and meat above. Next to the smoker, the lineup includes a gas-fired barbecue and griddle, a gas ring for a wok, and a sink. Design: Dietmar Kruger.

Outdoor Cooking Made Easy

Cradled in the curve of the gazebo's low brick retaining wall, this arc-shaped counter houses a gas-fired barbecue, a double sink with garbage disposer, a refrigerator, and custom storage cabinets. Landscape architect: Forsum/Summers & Partners.

Moving the Kitchen Outdoors

Family cookouts and company entertaining have long focused on the barbecue. It may still sit outside the back door, but increasingly, it has permanent companions—in some cases, the full range of comforts and conveniences found in standard indoor kitchens.

The four patio kitchens shown on these pages are located in Southern California, where the climate lends itself year-round to outdoor cooking and dining. But they can inspire homeowners even where outdoor living is more seasonal.

Layout and choice of cooking elements arise from each homeowner's favorite recipes and cooking techniques—from classic grilled steak and home-smoked salmon to stir-fried vegetables and griddle-cooked shrimp. Facilities built around the barbecue may include preparation and serving areas, storage cabinets, a refrigerator, a sink (sometimes equipped with a garbage disposer), and a place to eat.

Keeping outdoor cooking facilities clean poses a special problem. The kitchens shown here were designed to require little maintenance. Using protective grill covers and such rugged materials as concrete and tile makes it possible to clean the areas simply by hosing them down. Moisture-sensitive electrical outlets are placed out of the way of routine cleanup.

Most outdoor kitchens are at least partially sheltered by a patio roof (either freestanding or house attached) or by a gazebo.

Effective downlighting illuminates preparation areas; more diffuse fixtures, perhaps on a dimmer, create the ambience desired for a dinner party. (For more details on your lighting options, see pages 47–49.)

In order to install an outdoor kitchen, water supply pipes, drainpipes, and electrical cable or conduit must to be routed to your patio—beneath the slab if the patio is detached or, if the patio is attached to the house, via an exterior wall or overhead. In cold climates, pipes must be insulated or equipped with valves at low points to facilitate draining in winter. Drainpipes must be sloped toward the main drain, which is sometimes logistically difficult given the existing drainage layout.

Outdoor electrical outlets, light fixtures, and switches should be protected by watertight boxes; all outdoor outlets must also be protected by a ground fault circuit interrupter (GFCI), which shuts off power to the circuit in case of a short.

If you're planning an extensive kitchen addition outside, it's best to consult a landscape architect or contractor familiar with such additions.

Lighting Up the Night

Good outdoor lighting is both functional and esthetic. It's functional because it will give you the
right kind of light when you need it for entertaining, outdoor cooking, or a lively evening volleyball
game. It's esthetic because it will add to the beauty
of your outdoor space by highlighting architectural
elements and garden plantings.

Low voltage or standard current? Because they're
safer, more energy-efficient, and easier to install
than standard 120-volt systems, low-voltage lights
are often used outdoors. Such systems use a transformer to step down standard household current to
12 volts. (For help with installation, see pages
118–119.)

But the standard 120-volt system still has some
advantages outdoors. The buried cable and metallic
fixtures give the installation a look of permanence,
light can be projected a greater distance, and the
120-volt outlets accept standard power tools and
patio heaters.

Fixtures and bulbs. Useful outdoor fixtures include
well lights and other portable uplights for accenting
or silhouetting foliage, spread lights for illuminating
paths or bridges, and downlights for pinpointing
special garden features.

Most outdoor fixtures are made of bronze, cast
or extruded aluminum, copper, or plastic, but you
can also find decorative stone, concrete, and wood
fixtures (redwood, cedar, and teak weather best).
Size varies. When evaluating fixtures, look for gas-
kets, high-quality components at joints and pivot
points, and locking devices for aiming the fixture.

Choose the bulb and effect you want first and
then the appropriate fixtures. Low-voltage halogen
MR-16 bulbs are popular for accenting; PAR spotlights, available in both low and standard voltage,
are best to light trees or wide areas. Today's fluores-
cent bulbs are popular for outdoor use; both their
shape and their color rendition are superior to older
types.

Avoiding glare. Because the contrast between dark-
ness and a light source is so great, glare can be a big
problem at night. Keep the following points in mind
when you're planning your outdoor installation.

■ *Use shielded fixtures.* With a shielded light fixture, the bulb area is completely hidden by an
opaque covering that directs light away from the
viewer's eyes. Instead of a hot spot of light, the eye
sees the warm glow of the lighted object.

■ *Place fixtures out of sight lines,* either very low
(as along a walk) or very high. By doing that, you

Cookout Counter with a Water View
*Cool blue tiles surround the stainless steel sink and gas grill in
this 2-foot-deep barbecue counter. Tiles partially cover the sides
as well as the top of the counter, making the surface easy to
clean. Design: Patrick Evan Sheehy.*

Patio Cooking Oriental-style
*A weatherproof griddle, two gas barbecues, a pair of gas
burners, and ample storage units are built into this outdoor
kitchen. The serving counter is just the right height for seated
diners. Design: Jo Ann Messina/Fortner Millwork.*

These sculptural fixtures for lighting paths and walkways are meant to be seen. The three largest ones use standard voltage; the others

can direct them in such a way that only the light playing on the tree branches, and not a bright spot, is noticed.

■ *Lower light levels* by using several softer lights strategically placed around the patio and yard rather than one high-wattage light. A little light goes a long way at night: 20 watts is considered strong, and even 12 watts can be very bright. If you're using line current, choose bulbs with a 50-watt maximum.

Layering light levels. At night, the view outside ends where the light ends. To create depth, divide the landscape into three zones: a foreground, which has midlevel brightness; a softer middle ground; and a bright background to draw the eye through the garden.

Don't forget the view from inside, either. To avoid a "black hole" effect, strive to balance light levels on both sides of a window or sliding doors.

Extending a Warm Welcome

The view at night used to stop at the sliding glass doors. Now, the indoors is extended to the outside with MR-16 downlights that paint the courtyard patio. A waterproof PAR-36 fixture lights the garden pool from within, and movable MR-16 uplights spotlight the hanging baskets, the tree, and the plantings along the wall. Lighting design: Epifanio Juarez Design.

require low-voltage bulbs. The one at far left is teak, the one at far right redwood, and the rest metal or plastic.

Lighting for atmosphere and safety. On patios, a low level of light is often enough for quiet conversation or alfresco dining. Add stronger light for serving or barbecuing areas; downlights are popular, but indirect lighting, diffused through plastic or another translucent material, is also useful.

Illuminating foliage can be an effective way to combine functional and decorative lighting. For a dappled, moonlight effect, place both uplights and downlights in a large tree. To silhouette a tree or shrub, aim a spotlight or wall washer at a fence or wall from close behind the plant. Decorative mini-lights help outline trees and lend sparkle to your garden. Placing the lights on separate switches and installing dimmers adds flexibility.

Strings of mini-lights are also useful for lighting steps, railings, and walkways. Note that such areas are safest and easiest to illuminate if their surfaces are a light, reflective color. Low fixtures that spread soft pools of light along the walk can both show the way and highlight your garden's virtues. If your house has deep eaves or an overhang extending the length of the walk, consider weatherproof downlights that will illuminate your walk without the fixtures being visible.

Lighting pools, spas, and fountains. Most swimming pools have an underwater light in the deep end. To avoid glare, consider putting the light on a dimmer, especially if it's within view of the house or patio sitting area. For relaxing and entertaining around the pool, all that's needed is a soft glow to outline the pool edges, but the light should be on full brightness for swimmers. When the pool light is off, low spotlights reflecting on the surface of the water can provide a dramatic lighting effect.

Popular for an evening soak, a spa or hot tub can be illuminated with low-voltage twinkling mini-lights that will subtly outline its perimeter or steps.

Garden fountain units often come with their own integral lighting schemes. Sometimes optional filter kits for changing colors are included. Lights for garden pools are usually designed to be recessed in the concrete wall of the pool. You can also purchase portable lights equipped with lead plates that keep them on the pool or stream bottom; move these around to provide dramatic accent of a waterfall or plantings.

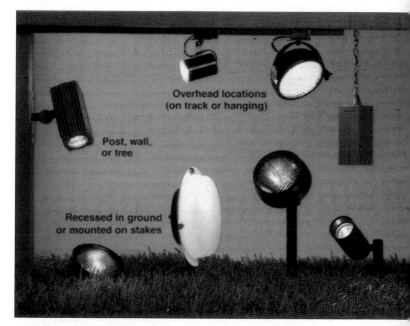

Overhead locations (on track or hanging)

Post, wall, or tree

Recessed in ground or mounted on stakes

Uplights, Downlights

These low-voltage fixtures aren't as flashy as the ones at the top of the page, but they handle uplighting and downlighting chores. Some can be sunk into the ground or mounted on stakes. Others can be secured to walls or large trees, suspended from tracks on patio roofs or trellises, or hung from tree branches.

Controlling Your Climate

A patio that receives too much sun or wind can have its climate modified in many ways. Overheads and trees protect patios from sun; screens moderate the effects of gusty winds. But to get the most out of your patio, you may want to consider adding some type of heating or cooling to take the edge off the temperature.

When you need heat. Fire pits or rings, which often double as barbecues, are good sources of heat. If you want to be able to move the fire around, try a low, round metal brazier—or more than one to help distribute the heat evenly. If your patio can accommodate it, consider including a full-scale fireplace.

Portable pottery fireplaces produce generous amounts of heat from only a small fire. But use them cautiously: they're lightweight and reasonably fragile, and they may break if the fire inside is too hot. You'll get the best results by burning kindling-size wood.

Remember that any open fire is a potential hazard. Be sure your fire is away from tree branches or patio overheads that could be ignited by flying sparks. Watch, too, for firebrands that may snap out onto decks and furniture; and on windy evenings, cover your fire with a fine wire mesh.

Taming the Heat

Growing ferns in a west-facing patio in California's hot Central Valley may sound like an impossible task, but here's the proof. The U-shaped house wraps around three sides of this courtyard; the entire area is roofed with lattice. An automatic misting system built into the overhead structure waters the plants and helps cool the surroundings.

Pull Up a Chair

A concrete slump-block fire pit is the focal point of this patio; it's part of a modular design that includes concrete aggregate paving squares trimmed with redwood dividers and a low wall that matches the fire pit. A roof overhang partially shades the expansive patio. Architect: MLA/Architects.

Gas-fed, butane, and electric infrared heaters, both portable and permanent, are also effective warmers. They emit primarily infrared rays, reflecting them downward and out to warm people and objects, rather than the air. They work best in sheltered areas.

Ideas for cooling. If soaring summertime temperatures keep you indoors more than out, you can benefit from a patio plan that incorporates one or more of the following cooling methods.

■ *Cooling with water.* Although garden pools, fountains, and waterfalls often appear in patio schemes for esthetic reasons, water also adds moisture to the air and helps cool a hot summer day. Even a simple garden sprinkler can reduce temperatures by 10 to 20 degrees. Summer breezes blowing across a garden pool absorb moisture and become cooler, as does the air around small spray fountains.

To add moisture to the air without installing a garden pool, consider using a mister, a type of spray head available at garden and irrigation supply stores; it throws a fine fog over moisture-loving plants. Often, a mister can be easily attached to a patio overhead or garden wall. Because misters use a minimum of water (some only 3 gallons per hour),

they can be operated constantly without creating drainage problems.

■ *Cooling with plants.* Shading with shrubs, trees, and vines may be your best solution to summer heat. Exposed to the sun, plant foliage absorbs, reflects, and reradiates heat efficiently without overheating the area it protects. Although plants raise the humidity of the surrounding air, the end result is a reduction in air temperature (unless the air is near the saturation point).

If you live in a mild climate, the filtered shade you get from a birch or olive tree may be enough; in hotter climates, you may need the denser foliage of a fruitless mulberry or sycamore. Be sure, however, that the plants you choose are not so dense that they block essential air movement.

■ *Cooling with air circulation.* Free circulation of air is another effective defense against summer heat, especially in hot, humid climates. If you're fortunate enough to have a prevailing summer breeze, plan your garden trees, shrubs, and fences to facilitate its passage across your patio. If summer air is still, keep shelter structures open to avoid creating a heat trap. Hanging fans add both air movement and pizzazz to an outdoor enclosure.

Including a Spa or Hot Tub

Common features in many gardens, spas and hot tubs have understandable appeal: an invigorating bath alfresco, usually enlivened by venturi jets, in a vessel large enough to accommodate both social and solitary soaks with equal aplomb.

Increasingly, spas also double as decorative water features in today's landscaping schemes. Waterfalls, fountain jets, formal tile or natural stone linings and borders, and exit streams meandering to the swimming pool are all ways to link the spa with the landscaping—and with surrounding features.

Once you've decided to add a spa or tub, you're faced with numerous design decisions. For help, look through home improvement magazines, visit the homes of friends or neighbors who have spas, or consult a spa dealer.

Spa or hot tub? Spas and tubs differ principally in material and form, not function. Spas are usually made of fiberglass or acrylic, or are custom-built of shotcrete or gunite. The molding technique used to manufacture spas makes possible nearly every conceivable shape—and such amenities as contoured built-in seats and changes in depth.

Although spas are rigid, they're not self-supporting; they must be set in sand, which is, in turn, held in place by stable earth or rigid retaining walls. Custom-built concrete spas are usually included as adjuncts to swimming pools and are built at the same time as the pool.

Hot tubs are made of wood in the manner of large, usually straight-sided barrels. With the proper foundation, tubs are self-supporting, so they're usually easier and less expensive to install than spas. Tubs must be sited so that air circulates around their sides and bottom; this retards the decay to which wood is prone.

Spas are most easily added below grade, which makes them suitable for patios and terraces. Above grade, spas must be surrounded by retaining walls to contain the supporting sand. Tubs are easy to install above grade; often a deck is added at or just below the edge of the tub for lounging.

Either a spa or a tub can be installed on a ledge cut into a hillside. In each case, a retaining wall is needed: on the downhill side for a spa, on the uphill side for a tub.

Choosing the best site. A number of practical considerations enter into your choice of site. Here are some of the most important.

■ *Microclimate.* You're probably already familiar with sun and wind patterns in your yard, but now is a good time to take a careful look. Try to anticipate when you're likely to use the spa or tub; then find one or more sites where sun and wind will be to your liking at that time of the day. At this point, you can begin to consider overheads (see pages 38–39) and screens (see pages 41–43).

■ *Proximity to house.* If the spa or tub will be the hub of social gatherings or if you plan to use it at night before retiring, you'll probably want to locate it near or on a patio or deck attached to the house. On the other hand, consider a site away from the house—perhaps an odd, unused corner of your lot—if you want seclusion or a second social area.

A Private Retreat

Bright with Victorian charm, this custom-made gazebo establishes visual boundaries for the tiled spa it encloses. It also provides privacy for bathers in a neighborhood with two-story houses without sacrificing the feeling of being outdoors. Gazebo design: Charles Lemmonier, Gazebo Nostalgia.

Dressing Up with Tile

This elegant spa, which doubles as a formal garden pool, is made from a concrete shell capped with hand-painted Spanish tile. Matching tile inlays in the Mexican paver border echo the cross-shaped motif. Landscape architect: Jeff Stone Associates.

■ *Privacy.* You'll probably feel more comfortable in a spa or tub if you're well screened from passersby. Overheads, gazebos, and screens—and even outdoor rooms (see page 43)—are often pressed into service for this purpose.

■ *Access.* Regardless of where the spa or tub is located with respect to the house, you'll need to provide a way of getting there that's comfortable, even for bare feet. You'll probably want a paved walk from the house, plus masonry or wood paving around the spa or tub itself.

■ *Local codes.* Like a swimming pool, local laws regard a spa or tub as an attractive nuisance. Consult local zoning ordinances regarding covers, fencing requirements, setback limits, and other rules. You'll also need a building permit. Spas and tubs must have secure covers to keep children out of the water when they are not being supervised.

Equipment and utilities. Siting is, to some extent, governed by plumbing. Heaters, pumps, and filters are compact, but they do take up space and require connections to electrical and gas lines. The expense of running these lines may also limit your choice of location. If you're using solar heating panels, you'll need to find a place for them, usually on the roof; this may dictate a site near the house.

Home for a Hot Tub

A classic hot tub snugs into one of a series of low-level decks built from garden grades of redwood. The deck provides a spot for lounging, facilitates drainage, and allows the tub to be installed above grade. Tile paving complements the woodsy redwood palette. Design: Jim Babcock.

Patio Oasis

This natural-looking garden pool is a focal point of a "dry" landscape, providing the cooling effect—and the reflective magic—of still water to the surrounding patio area. The paving is a mosaic of small river rock and larger fieldstones set in concrete; flagstones mark the pool's edges.

Wall of Water

Surprise! Fountains do not issue only from the mouths of frogs or the jugs of milk maidens. This one was built into a concrete block and stucco wall when the house was constructed. The steep fountain ramp is lined with Saltillo pavers; water is recycled through a recirculating pump. Landscape architect: Deweese/Burton Associates.

Flagstone Terrace

After a number of meandering turns and spills, this flagstone-lined stream makes its way to a collecting pool near the bottom of the terraced courtyard. At night, each cascade is illuminated by a portable, sealed fixture—one is visible in the stream channel at center. Architect: The Steinberg Group. Landscape architect: Eldon Beck Associates.

Garden Fountains & Pools

Adding moving water to your patio environment both introduces a cooling effect and provides a barrier against unwanted outside noises. Even if cooling and noise aren't problems, you still may want to include a garden pool or fountain for esthetic reasons, or to indulge a penchant for growing water plants or raising koi.

If you decide to add a garden pool to your landscape, consult a landscape professional for design ideas.

Fountains. Water in motion is nearly always dramatic, and the simplest fountain can add a musical dimension to the smallest patio or deck.

Garden fountains usually fall into one of three categories. *Spray* fountains are made versatile by assorted fountain heads that send water upward in shapes ranging from massive columns to lacy mists. *Spill*, or *wall*, fountains send a single stream of water falling into a pool or series of tiered pans or shelves. *Splash* fountains, which are almost always profes-

sionally designed, force water up through a piece of sculpture.

Garden pools. The size and shape of a garden pool is limited only by your imagination and your space. A still-water garden pool can be small and decorative or complex and natural, depending on the effect you wish. For do-it-yourselfers, the only rule is this: keep it simple. Complex designs not only are difficult to manage during construction but also rarely achieve the hoped-for effect.

■ *Accent pools.* If you want to start small, consider the tiny portable decorative pools available at garden supply stores and statuary stores. Or search your home for something you can convert to a small outdoor pool.

Another possibility is a tub garden. You'll need only a few springtime hours and some simple ingredients: a waterproof container that holds at least 25 gallons, some bog or aquatic plants (water lilies are a favorite), and a few goldfish to help keep the pool clean. Tub garden "finds" include ceramic planters, wine barrels, and claw-foot bathtubs.

Weathering the Elements

Teak furniture stands up to nasty weather. Chairs, small tables, and container plants can all be repositioned for maximum flexibility. Landscape architect: R. David Adams Associates, Inc.

A Swinging Patio

Hanging bench swing provides a resting spot in this courtyard nestled between the house and the garage. The swing is sturdily anchored to a beam on the wisteria-clad patio roof.

■ *Formal pools.* Traditional garden pools, made of brick, concrete, fitted stone, or tile, often blend as easily into contemporary patio settings as they do into formal surroundings. They also offer a fine opportunity to introduce color and texture through the use of such aquatic plants as water lilies and floating hyacinths. A raised pool with brick walls provides a classic home for goldfish and koi.

■ *Natural pools.* Although natural-looking pools, streams, and waterfalls are the most enjoyable to create, they demand the most sensitive design and maintenance, as well as a natural setting.

A natural-appearing pool is almost any body of water that doesn't have square corners, perpendicular walls, or man-made edges. Most older natural pools are hand-packed shells made of reinforced concrete; today, do-it-yourselfers may opt for pool liners or fiberglass shells (see pages 142–143 for details).

Pumps, filters, and other hardware. A simple pool pump can supply a stream, waterfall, or fountain, aerate the water, and power a filter system.

Filters for garden pools run the gamut from simple strainer baskets to swimming pool filters to custom-built biological filters for large koi ponds. For a small garden pool that has no plants or fish, chemical filtration—algicides and other water-clearing agents—is often the best choice.

Installing a drain in your pool makes maintenance easier. If you need to keep a constant water level, install a float valve, either a special pool model or the toilet-bowl type.

Storage

Storage systems on or near your patio keep equipment and supplies close to where you need them.

Some of the best ideas are the simplest, such as patio benches that open up to store cushions or sports equipment, or cabinets that are attached to an existing wall for barbecue paraphernalia. Perhaps a storage closet with an access door can be built into a garage wall framing the patio. A low-level deck might allow for a trap door to a lined, excavated space below. Or you can make use of space beneath an adjacent raised deck.

Most small-scale storage units are easy to build and are portable. Larger units—permanent or portable, freestanding or attached to an existing structure—can double as screens to divide the patio from a garden work center. When designed to harmonize with the garden, they blend into the landscape. Before you build a large storage unit or position a prefabricated shelter, check local building codes and ordinances.

Furniture

When you select outdoor furniture, your first concern should be comfort—but keep an eye out for durability as well. Outdoor furniture can take a beating from the elements; though often expensive, furniture designed and built to withstand weather is more economical in the long run.

Most standard garden furniture is constructed of aluminum, wrought iron, steel, or wood. If you live in a damp climate, painted or enameled aluminum-frame furniture is a good choice because it won't rust. Rust can scar wrought-iron and steel furniture if the paint adheres poorly. (Ask your furniture dealer about rust-resistant coatings for any steel or wrought-iron furniture you're considering purchasing.)

Although generally not as durable as standard furnishings, folding and collapsible garden furniture stacks for easy storage and can be useful when you need extra seating. Many people like wood-framed director's chairs with canvas seats and backs because they're comfortable, good-looking, colorful, and usually reasonably priced. The canvas will eventually deteriorate, but it's easily replaced.

Often cumbersome and weighty, wood garden furniture belongs where it doesn't need to be moved frequently. Another disadvantage to wood is that it often splinters with age. In the West, redwood is a relatively inexpensive and popular material for standard garden furniture, but it's scarce and costly in other areas. Cedar heartwood shares redwood's warm color and durability. Teak, though relatively expensive, is popular for wooden benches, tables, and chairs. Quality teak weathers to a distinguished gray color and tolerates moisture admirably.

Combining built-in and movable furniture is a good solution for homeowners who want to use their patios year-round, but who must store garden chairs in winter. Built-in perimeter benches frequently find a place in patio and deck designs because of their versatility: they serve as overflow seating when you entertain, buffet counters for outdoor suppers, platforms for container plants, railings near level changes, and seating on sunny winter days (keep a supply of cushions handy to make them more comfortable). Because they provide maximum seating in a minimum space, built-in benches are excellent for small gardens.

Decay-resistant softwood is the most popular material for built-in seats and underpinnings. Support structures are also made of metal, brick, concrete, or stone. Any material used for edgings or raised beds can support a perimeter bench—just widen the top and add a seat. For pointers on designing and building your own benches, see pages 130–131.

Secluded Alcove

A pea-gravel path and trimmed boxwood hedge lead the way to a private patio nook complete with stone bench. 'Beauty Bush' drapes its profuse blossoms over the scene.

On the Waterfront

Wood slats form the seat and back of this built-in bench; the stone facing adds a look of permanence. Landscape architect: R. David Adams Associates, Inc.

Ringed by Roses

Thanks to a mass planting of the floribunda-shrub rose 'Simplicity', this patio enclosure is colorful throughout the growing season. The flagstone paving with its mossy joints contributes to the mood.

Landscaping a Patio

Within the larger framework of any landscape design, a patio is a perfect stage for showing off beautiful plants. When placed against a simple background, pots of bright annuals splash color across a patio. Roses and vining plants can climb over many types of patio overheads. Where ground space is limited, plants can hang overhead or on walls. Patio plantings can also screen against wind or sun, disguise structural elements, and liven up drab corners or flat expanses of paving.

Containers. Containers can bring annuals and perennials, shrubs, and even vegetables to any location you wish on your patio surface. To get shade where there is none, bring on a tree in a half-barrel or tub. If you enjoy gardening, you can give your patio a new look by changing container plants to display the best of each season. Containers also allow ten-der plants to winter-over in a sheltered spot or on a sunny porch (trays with casters underneath the containers make moving them easy).

In formal landscapes, colorful masonry or wooden planters can accentuate the symmetrical placement and shaping of permanent plantings. Raised beds are the most formal planters; they raise plants to a comfortable viewing height.

Hanging pots and baskets. Hanging plants not only provide interesting texture and colorful accents, but also serve as shade and shelter if they're thick enough. When plants are suspended from the beams or joists of an open patio roof, they open up the floor space below them, allowing you to make the most of a small patio. For efficient watering, plan to run drip tubing and spray emitters to the pots from above.

If you don't have an overhead structure, or if the headroom isn't sufficient for hanging plants, try baskets and built-in containers mounted to an adjacent house wall; or construct a lattice or metal screen and grow a "wall" of plants on it.

Plant pockets and crazy paving. There's no rule saying that plants must be confined to containers. It's a simple matter when planning your patio to leave out a few units of masonry paving or to block off an open area on a concrete pour. When construction is completed, plants can be fitted into the empty spaces.

Another traditional idea that creates a cottage-garden feel is crazy paving—interspersing mosses, ground covers, or other low-lying plants among masonry units. You can even drill through concrete paving to route drip tubing to feed your new crevice plantings a small, steady diet.

Containers on the Move

A container garden of varied plantings commands this patio corner; portable planters and pots provide colorful accents and can be repositioned as the sun—and seasons—dictate.

All in Order

Radiating arcs of herbs and potted lemons are a sight to behold, and only a short walk for the cook: the door to the kitchen is located right next to the main brick patio. Design: Cynthia Woodyard.

PLANNING YOUR PATIO

L earning about the various styles, materials, and special features available for patios, as shown in the first two chapters, is only the first step toward achieving the environment you want to create. Even if you have a good idea of the basic patio style and elements you want, you need to take the crucial next step— focusing in on the perfect site for the patio and putting all your ideas down on paper.

This chapter begins with a look at basic design considerations and reviews some important site factors you should be aware of—sun, wind, rain, snow, and microclimates. Next comes the hands-on design process—from mapping your property, through sketching and experimenting, to polishing up your final plan. Along the way, we'll discuss general guidelines for good design. Helpful hints for dealing with building codes and variances, and descriptions of the professionals who can help you, close out the chapter.

Need specific examples for inspiration? Turn to pages 76–79 to see how landscape architects and designers made over the same typical lots—maybe one like yours.

It All Ties Together

Careful design yields this formal entry courtyard. The seeded-aggregate concrete paving with brick dividers leads to the front door; the brick motif is repeated along planting borders, in raised beds, and in the wall fountain's trim. Landscape architect: Robert Chittock.

Getting Started

Focus first on your family's needs and habits. Think about the way you live, making a list of what's most important to you (if you have children, get their input, too); then, if you need to compromise, you can compromise on the less important things.

Consider your lifestyle. Do you like to entertain frequently outdoors, and, if so, do you prefer casual or formal entertaining? Do the neighborhood kids always seem to congregate in your yard? How much time do you want to spend gardening and maintaining your yard? Do you have pets that might damage fragile patio plants or furniture? Your answers to those questions will determine some basic design elements for your patio.

Next, evaluate your yard's assets and liabilities. Even if you plan to enlist the services of a landscape architect, designer, or other professional (see page 75), you need to have a good understanding of your existing landscape.

Can your patio plan capitalize on a fine view? Is your property bounded by woods? Perhaps your design can take advantage of a sunny southern exposure, mature plantings, or an impressive garden tree.

Consider also your yard's handicaps. Is your lot on a steep slope? How much of the lot is exposed to street traffic and noise? Is humidity a problem in your area during the summer months? Does your present patio open off the wrong room, get too much sun or shade, or lack sufficient space? You'll want to plan a patio that minimizes your yard's special problems.

The exact location of your patio will depend largely on the size and contour of your lot, the way your house sits on it, the uses you have in mind for the patio, and your climate. A number of different sites and configurations are shown below. For even more possibilities, browse through the text and photos in the first chapter.

Understanding Weather

Understanding the climate around your home is important in patio planning. If you know what to expect from the weather around you, you can plan a

A Potpourri of Patio Sites

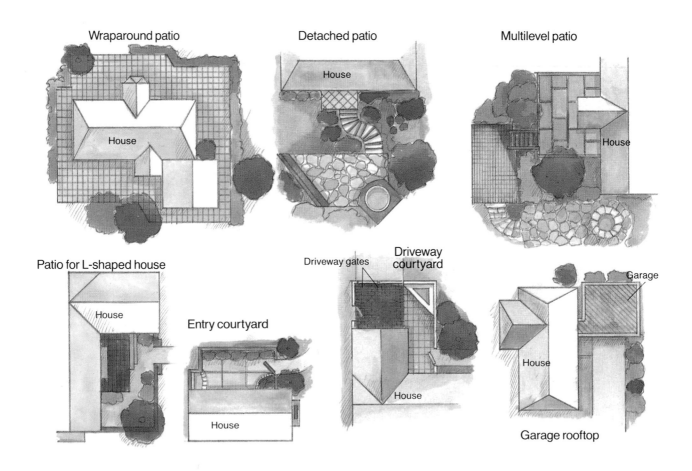

Wraparound patio

Detached patio

Multilevel patio

Patio for L-shaped house

Entry courtyard

Driveway gates

Driveway courtyard

Garage

Garage rooftop

patio that will be enjoyable over a longer outdoor season.

If you've lived in your present home for a number of seasons, you're already familiar with your climate's benefits and hazards. But if you're new to the area, you may want to obtain accurate information to help you get acquainted with general weather patterns. Such information is available from local U.S. Weather Bureau offices, public power or utility companies, meteorology departments on college and university campuses, and county agricultural extension offices.

Your Relation to the Sun

A patio's exposure to sun is one of the most important factors in your enjoyment of the space. Knowing the sun's path over your property may prompt you to adjust the site of your proposed patio, extend its dimensions, or change its design in order to add a few weeks or months of sun or shade to your outdoor room. Often, you can moderate the effects of the sun with the addition of a patio roof.

Basic orientation. Theoretically, a patio that faces north is cold because it rarely receives the sun. A south-facing patio is usually warm because, from sunrise to sunset, the sun never leaves it. A patio on the east side is cool, receiving only morning sun. And a west-facing patio is often unbearably hot because it receives the full force of the sun's midafternoon rays; in addition, late afternoon sun often creates a harsh glare.

Generally, your patio temperature will follow this north-south-east-west rule. Exceptions do occur in climates where extreme summer or winter temperatures are predictable. For example, mid-July temperatures in Phoenix, Arizona, often climb above 100° F., and a north-facing patio there could hardly be considered "cold." In San Francisco, on the other hand, a patio with a southern or western exposure could hardly be considered hot because stiff ocean breezes and chilly fogs are common during the summer months.

Seasonal path of the sun. Another factor to consider is the sun's path during the year (see the drawing below). As the sun passes over your house, it

Plotting the Sun's Path

Season	Sun's Position/Hours of Daylight		
	Area I	Area II	Area III
Noon, 12/21	21°/8 hrs.	29°/9 hrs.	37°/10 hrs.
Noon, 3/21 & 9/21	45°/12 hrs.	53°/12 hrs.	60°/12 hrs.
Noon, 6/21	69°/16 hrs.	76°/15 hrs.	83°/14 hrs.

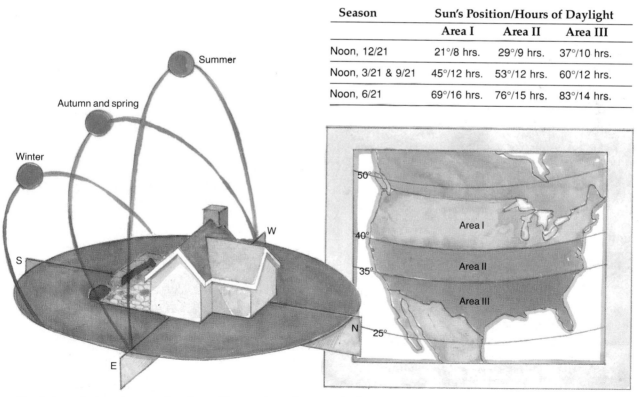

Shade is cast at various angles, depending on time of year and where you live. Find your location on map at right; then refer to chart for sun angles and hours of daylight on your property.

makes an arc that changes slightly every day, becoming higher in summer and lower in winter. Changes in the sun's path give us long days in summer and short ones in winter, and they also alter sun and shade patterns on your patio. Find your location on the map on page 63; refer to the chart just above the map for sun angles and hours of daylight on your property.

Battling Wind, Rain & Snow

Like sun, wind can be a major foe—or ally—affecting patio comfort and enjoyment. Rain and snow, though admittedly more foreboding, can also be neutralized to some degree by careful planning.

Understanding wind. Study the wind patterns around your house and over your lot. Too much wind blowing across your patio on a cool day can be just as unpleasant as no breeze at all on a hot day. Evaluating the wind will help you discover how to control or encourage it with fences, screens, or plants.

Three different kinds of winds can affect your site: annual prevailing winds, very localized seasonal breezes (daily, late afternoon, or summer), and occasional high-velocity winds generated by stormy weather.

Although you can determine the prevailing winds in your neighborhood by noticing the direction the trees lean, chances are that the prevailing winds around your house are different. Wind flows like water, spilling over obstacles, breaking into currents, eddying and twisting. After blowing through the trees, the wind may spill over the house and drop onto your patio.

If you're considering building a screen or fence to block wind from blowing across your patio, note that different wind barriers create different effects, as shown in the wind-control study at right. The illustration indicates that solid barriers aren't necessarily the best ones.

To determine the screen or fence that's best suited for your situation, pinpoint the wind currents in your yard. Post small flags where you want wind protection and note their movements during windy periods.

Dealing with rain and snow. If, in assessing your climate, you learn that winter storms generally blow out of the northeast, you may want to locate your patio where it will take less of a beating from the weather—perhaps on the south side of the house where it will be partially protected by trees or a roof overhang.

If you live in an area frequented by brief summer cloudbursts, you can extend the patio's

Wind Direction/Fence Height

Solid vertical barrier
Protection drops off at a distance roughly equal to barrier's height

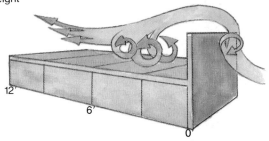

Spaced-wood screen
Wind diffused near screen, with best protection 6'–12' from barrier

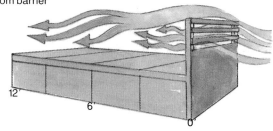

Solid barrier, baffle angled into wind
Good protection near barrier and to a distance more than twice barrier's height

Solid barrier, baffle angled toward patio
Best protection up to 8' from barrier

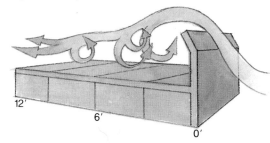

Wind-control studies indicate that a solid vertical screen or fence isn't necessarily the best barrier against wind. Lattice-type screening provides diffused protection near fence; fence-top baffle aimed into wind offers the most shelter.

Microclimates

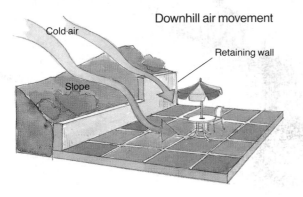

Downhill air movement

Cold air

Slope

Retaining wall

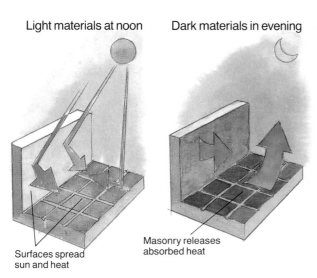

Light materials at noon

Dark materials in evening

Surfaces spread
sun and heat

Masonry releases
absorbed heat

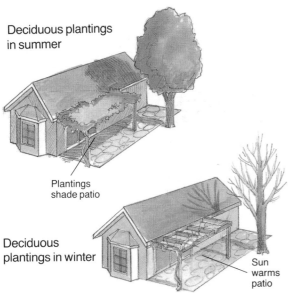

Deciduous plantings
in summer

Plantings
shade patio

Deciduous
plantings in winter

Sun
warms
patio

*Microclimates affect patio comfort, as shown. Cold air
flows downhill and may be dammed by a wall or house
(at top); light-colored materials reflect light and heat,
dark colors absorb it (center); deciduous plantings shade
in summer, allow winter sun to penetrate (at bottom).*

usefulness with a solid roof (see pages 38–39) that
lets you sit outdoors during warm-weather rains.
Since it's easiest to lay the foundation for the roof at
the same time that you build the patio, advance
planning is a must. If you're located in snow
country, be sure whatever overhead design you
choose can handle snow and ice buildup.

Your Property's Microclimate

Probably no one experiences exactly the same
temperature as the weather bureau. A reported
temperature of 68° F. means that a thermometer in
the shade, protected from the wind, reads 68° F. If
there's a 10- to 15-mile-an-hour breeze, a person in
the shade will feel that the temperature is about 62°
F., while someone on a sunny patio sheltered from
the breeze will feel a comfortable 75° to 78° F.

This is an illustration of microclimates—pockets
created by combinations of sun, exposure, and other
factors. Though sun and wind are major factors,
they're not the only ones. Several potential microclimates are shown in the drawings at left.

Remember that cold air flows downhill like
water, "puddles" in basins, and can also be dammed
by walls or solid fences. If you build a sunken patio
or one walled in by your house and a retaining wall
below house level, you may find yourself shivering
at sunset while higher surroundings are quite balmy.
Note any spots where cold air settles and frost is
heavy.

Keep in mind, too, that certain materials reflect
sun and/or heat better than others. For example,
light-colored masonry paving and walls are great for
spreading sun and heat, but they can be uncom-
fortably bright; wood surfaces are usually cooler. On
the other hand, dark masonry materials retain heat
a little longer, making evenings on your patio a little
warmer. Plants help block wind, but they let some
breezes through. Well-placed deciduous trees can
shelter a patio from hot sun in summer, yet allow
welcome rays to penetrate on crisp winter days.

Drawing a Base Map

The first step in turning your ideas and ideals into
reality is to take a long, careful look at what you
have right now. Even if you're remodeling a landscape you've lived with for years, this close exami-
nation is essential. In recording the necessary information objectively, accurately, and completely, you
may make startling discoveries about what you
thought was familiar.

Use your accumulated observations about your
site and its setting to create a base map, such as the

one shown on the facing page. Be as precise as possible; "guesstimates" or outright errors at this stage can result in disappointment later when, for example, you find that your new patio is in deep shade when you most want to use it.

To draw your base map (and later, your final plan), you'll need 24- by 36-inch graph paper (¼-inch scale, unless the size of your property requires ⅛-inch scale), an art gum eraser, a straightedge, several pencils, and a pad of tracing paper. Optional are a drafting board, a T-square, one or more triangles, a compass, a circle template, and an architect's scale. For measurements in the landscape itself, choose either a 50- or a 100-foot tape measure; anything shorter is exasperating to use and can lead to inaccurate measurements.

You can draw your base map directly on graph paper or on tracing paper placed over graph paper. If you plan to have a blueprinting company make copies of your base map, though, it will have to be drawn on tracing paper; a blueprint machine will not accept regular graph paper.

Starting with the dimensions of your property and proceeding through all the information listed here, you'll gradually be covering a good deal of your paper with written and sketched details, so make each entry as neat and concise as possible.

You can save yourself hours of measuring and data-gathering at this point by obtaining much of your information—from dimensions and orientation to relevant structural details and gradient—from your deed map, house plans, or a contour map of your lot. If you don't have these at hand, see if they're available at your city hall, county office, title company, bank, or mortgage company.

The specific information below should appear in one form or another on your base map.

■ *Boundary lines and dimensions.* Outline your property accurately and to scale, and mark its dimensions on the base map.

■ *The house.* Show your house precisely and to scale within the property. Note all doors to the outside and the direction that each one opens, the height above ground of all lower-story windows, and all overhangs.

Take time to evaluate the architectural style of your house; even if it fits no category neatly, you can probably establish its relative level of formality. What are its visual pluses and minuses? Later, you'll use this information to decide whether to camouflage or highlight particular aspects. At later planning stages, you'll want to keep attractive views open, maybe even accentuate them, and screen unattractive ones.

■ *Exposure.* Draw a north arrow, using a compass; then note on your base map the shaded and sunlit areas of your present landscape. Also note the microclimates—hot and cold spots and windy areas—that you'll want to take into account in designing your new landscape. Indicate the direction of the prevailing wind and any spots that are especially windy and may require protection of some sort.

■ *Utilities and easements.* Show on your map the locations of hose bibbs and the depths and locations of all underground lines, including the sewage line or septic tank. If you're contemplating planting tall trees or constructing a patio overhead or gazebo, show the locations and heights of all overhead lines.

If your deed map shows any easements, note them accurately on your base map and check legal restrictions limiting development of those areas.

■ *Downspouts and drain systems.* Mark the locations of all downspouts and any drainage tiles, drainpipes, or catch basins they drain into.

■ *Gradient.* Draw contour lines on your base map, noting high and low points (here's where the official contour map is helpful). If drainage crosses boundaries, you may need to indicate the gradient of adjacent properties as well, to ensure that you're not channeling runoff onto your neighbor's property.

For small, nearly level sites, you can measure slope with a level and a straight board, as shown on page 136. More complex jobs may call for a builder's transit—and the know-how to use it.

■ *Drainage.* Surface drainage, of course, corresponds to gradient. Where does the water from paved surfaces drain? Note where drainage is impeded at any point, leaving soil soggy, and whether runoff from a steep hillside is rapid enough to cause erosion.

■ *Existing plantings.* If you're remodeling an old landscape, note any existing plantings that you want to retain or that would require a major effort to remove.

■ *Views.* Note all views, attractive or unattractive, from every side of your property—they can affect the enjoyment of your patio. Also take into account views into your yard from neighboring houses or streets. While screens and overheads may be able to ensure some privacy, they may not impede views from neighbors' second-story windows. Note vantage points where relevant.

■ *The environs.* Step a bit further and consider some larger factors before completing your base map. What are the visual characteristics of your neighborhood? Are there prevailing landscape and architectural styles?

Finally, note on your base map the relation of the street and its traffic to your house.

Tools of the Trade

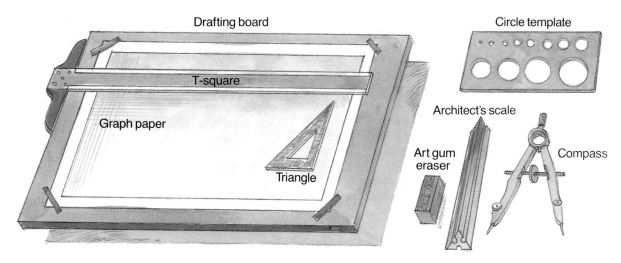

Bare-bones equipment for patio planning includes graph paper, pencils, eraser, and straightedge; additional drafting tools make the work go smoother and produce neater results.

A Sample Base Map

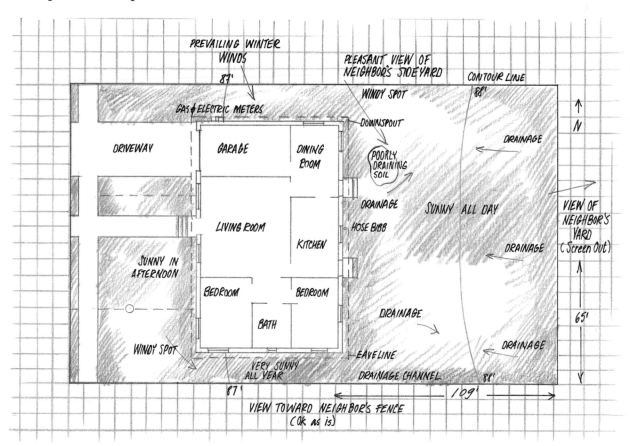

A preliminary step in any landscaping project is to make a base map—a scale drawing showing the important features and characteristics of the property. The drawing becomes the foundation on which the final patio plan is built.

Size Guidelines

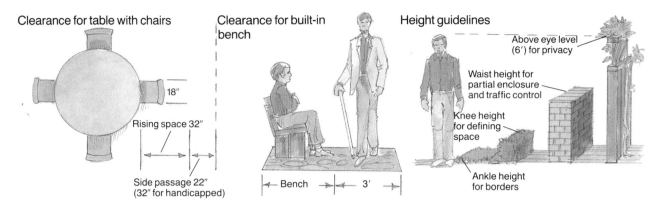

Clearance for table with chairs

18"

Rising space 32"

Side passage 22"
(32" for handicapped)

Clearance for built-in
bench

◄— Bench —►◄— 3' —►

Height guidelines

Above eye level
(6') for privacy

Waist height for
partial enclosure
and traffic control

Knee height
for defining
space

Ankle height
for borders

Four Landscaping Principles

Whatever landscape style you choose—formal,
freeform, or naturalistic—observing the four basic
landscaping principles will ensure that your patio is
a pleasure to behold. Through years of experience,
landscaping professionals have absorbed these
guidelines so completely that they never lose sight
of them throughout the design process.

It's a good idea to return to this section repeatedly as your plan develops; when your design is
complete, check back to make sure you haven't
forgotten or altered your original intentions amid
the flurry of other planning considerations.

Unity. Unity means that everything in your patio
looks like it belongs together: paving, overhead, and
screens complement each other; furniture suits the
patio's architectural style; and patio plants relate
both to each other and to plants in the garden.

Unity between patio and house is important,
too. If your patio is off a kitchen decorated in a
casual style, the patio should have the same feeling.

Variety. Variety keeps unity from becoming monotonous. Good design offers an element of surprise: a
path that leads from the main terrace to a more
intimate one, a plant display that makes a garden
work center part of the patio, a subtle wall fountain
that gives dimension to a small space, trees that
provide varying degrees of light and shade at
different times of day.

Variety also provides interest on a vertical
plane. Patios at different levels, low walls, raised
beds, privacy screens, and container plants of
varying heights help draw the eye away from a
horizontal expanse.

Proportion. Proportion demands that your patio
structure be in scale with your house and garden.

Remember that your patio is an outdoor, not an
indoor room, and there will be a difference in scale.
Though many patios are scaled to the size of the
living room, don't be afraid to design something
larger. Outdoor furniture generally takes up more
space than indoor furniture, and you may want
room for containers of plants. Keep in mind, too, the
range of activity you want your patio to be able to
accommodate.

There are sensible limits, however. If your lot is
so big that you need a large patio to keep everything
in scale, try creating smaller areas within the larger
whole. For example, squares of plantings inset in
paving will break up a monotonous surface; baffle
plantings or fences can divide one large area into
two or more functional spaces.

To maintain proportion in a small patio, keep
the design simple and uncluttered. Clean lines
make elements seem larger. Stepped planting beds
lead the eye up and out of a confined area. Tall
vertical screens used to enclose a small area actually
make it appear larger, as does such solid paving as
brick, with its small-scale, repetitive pattern.

If you have a small patio, use moderate-size
furniture (built-ins are especially effective) to avoid
a crowded feeling. Use plants with restraint—
overplanting just adds clutter. Remember to choose
plants with their ultimate sizes and shapes in mind.
Young poplar trees might suit the proportion of
your patio now, but within a few years they may
grow too tall for it.

Balance. Balance is achieved when design elements
are artfully combined to produce the same visual
weight (*not* symmetry) on either side of a center of
interest. If your patio is shaded on one side by a
mature tree, you can balance the tree's weight with
perimeter benches on the other side. If your patio is
small and enclosed, but equipped at one end with a
garden pool, try balancing the pool with patio
furniture and accent plants.

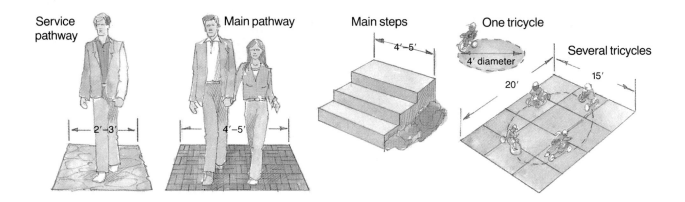

Service pathway — 2'–3'

Main pathway — 4'–5'

Main steps — 4'–5'

One tricycle — 4' diameter

Several tricycles — 20', 15'

Experimenting with Your Ideas

With your base map completed, you can now begin trying out your ideas and determining the style of your patio. As you sketch, you'll begin to work out use areas and circulation patterns, and to make general decisions about what kinds of plants and structures you'll need and where to place them.

Here are some tips to make the design process more effective:

■ *Sketch as many designs as you can*—at this stage, mistakes cost nothing. At some point during the process, your final design will crystallize, bringing with it a feeling of achievement.

■ *Think in three dimensions.* This will help you balance the design elements and visualize the results, and keep you from confining your design to an endless horizontal plane. Slide projector planning (see page 71) can help make this process simpler.

■ *Rely on familiar shapes.* Landscape designs based on squares, rectangles, circles, and hexagons almost always generate eye-pleasing results that you won't tire of quickly. Avoid arbitrarily curved patterns.

■ *Try to see your design as a whole.* Since your patio is part of both the garden and the house, it will have an impact on both. If, for instance, you plan a patio off the living room, shaded by an attached patio roof, will the roof make the living room too dark? Will your patio eliminate your children's play space?

■ *Test your ideas.* As you sketch, don't limit yourself to the abstract information on the base map. Experiment directly on the landscape by pacing off areas or using stakes or chairs to help visualize spaces and distances. Walk through contemplated traffic paths; bounce your ideas off others who know the site. Then modify your sketches as needed.

Defining use areas. Review and prioritize how you want to use your new patio. Will it be for entertaining, recreation, relaxation, storage, or some combination of these uses? Make a list and keep it before you as you draw.

For each design attempt, use a separate sheet of tracing paper placed over your base map, sketching "balloons"—rough circles or ovals—to represent the location and approximate size of each use area. For an example, see the drawing below.

A Balloon Sketch

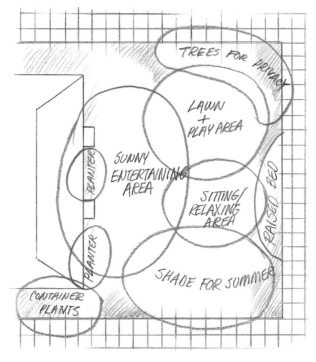

Place tracing paper over your base map; then sketch circles for use areas and other features.

As you draw, concentrate on logical placement and juxtaposition. Are you locating a children's play area in full view of your living area? Is the small, private space you envision easily accessible from the master bedroom? Do you really want a patio designed for entertaining guests located next to the service yard?

Plan generously—you can always cut back later if the plan becomes too costly. Creating a strong design now will help you distinguish between the more and less important elements of your plan, making later adjustments easier.

If you have doubts about the lay of the land, consult the information on grading and drainage on page 72.

Examining circulation patterns. Visualize foot-traffic connections between the various patio use areas, as well as to the house and yard. Will too much traffic be channeled through areas meant for relaxation? Can guests move easily from the entertainment area into the backyard? Consider whether the lawn mower or garden cart can be moved from the toolshed to the lawn without disturbing someone's repose. One way to improve access to and from the house is to add a door, as described on pages 110–111.

When planning pathways, steps, and other routes, you'll need to figure in at least the established minimum clearances; for guidelines, see the illustrations on pages 68–69.

Using color. Just as the colors of a beautiful room stand in a coordinated relationship to one another, so do they also in a lovely landscape.

Keep color in mind, then, as you choose materials for paving, overheads, walls, and screens. Brick, adobe, wood, and stone—materials commonly used for patios—have distinctive, generally earthy colors. And don't forget to take your house into account: since it's the most prominent feature of your landscape, the materials you're using on your patio should blend with its color.

Even plants on or around your patio should combine harmonious colors, representing a continuous segment of the color wheel: red, red violet, and violet, for example (see illustration at right). The smaller the area, the narrower the segment should be. Use complementary colors—those opposite one another on the color wheel—sparingly, for accents. Remember that all foliage is not simply "green"; the range of shades is actually quite large.

Choosing structural elements. Look closely at the successful patio designs shown in the first two chapters. What elements do you need to include to create your own ideal outdoor environment? What materials will you use? (Before deciding, you may

want to look through the information on building techniques on pages 81–137.)

As you begin to firm up your design, check off the following elements:

- *Paving material or combination of materials*

- *Edgings where appropriate*

- *Retaining walls for hilly or sloping lots*

- *Walkways and footpaths linking the patio to the house or to other parts of the yard*

- *Steps or formal stairs for changes in level*

- *Walls, fences, or screens for privacy and noise control*

- *Doors for access from the house*

Choosing amenities. Although some finishing touches, such as outdoor benches and planters, can be added later, now is the best time to think about the amenities you want and to sketch them on your design (for ideas and inspiration, turn to pages 37–59). If you think you may want to add outdoor lighting or perhaps a sink or wet bar to your outdoor living area later on, you need to plan now for the necessary wire or pipe runs.

The Color Wheel

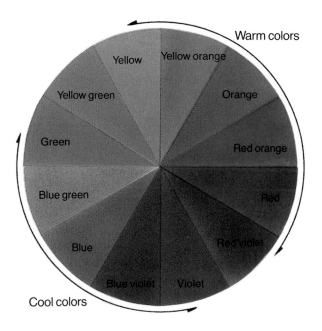

As a rule, work with adjacent colors on color wheel; save complementary colors—those opposite one another—for accents.

Here are items you should be considering now:

- *Patio roof or gazebo*
- *Garden pool, fountain, waterfall, or stream*
- *Spa or hot tub*
- *Barbecue area with kitchen facilities*
- *Fire pit*
- *Built-in benches or other furniture*
- *Outdoor lighting (120-volt or low-voltage 12-volt)*
- *Electrical outlets (GFCI-protected)*
- *Outdoor heater*
- *Hose bibb*
- *Raised beds for plants or built-in planters*

Designing the Modular Way

Sometimes it's helpful to work with a single unit of space—such as a square or rectangle—repeated over and over again like squares on a checkerboard. Uni-

A Modular Plan

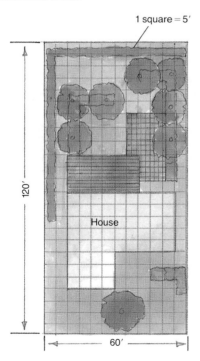

Divide your sketch into uniform-size modules; then lay out patio, walkways, planters, and other features in multiples of that unit.

form design units help you be more exact in preliminary planning and give a sense of order to your design. You'll also find modules helpful when estimating materials—just figure the materials for one mod and then count the units up to arrive at an overall total.

Modular planning is especially advantageous if you're laying patio paving for the first time. Concrete can be mixed and poured in rectangles or squares; bricks and other masonry units can be laid one rectangle at a time.

When designing a patio with modules, you can use a design unit of almost any size or shape. Most professionals suggest a module that's no less than 3 by 3 feet.

To find out what size you should use, measure the length of the house wall that adjoins your proposed patio site. If it's 24 feet long, six 4-foot rectangles will fit your wall dimension exactly. If you plan to work with brick, tile, or adobe blocks, make your module an exact multiple of their dimensions (be sure to include space for open joints if they're to be set in mortar).

Suppose, for example, you decide to work with a 5-foot square. The illustration below, at left, shows how your patio can be divided. The low-level deck is 15 by 30 feet (3 by 6 modules); the adjacent masonry patio is 15 by 25 feet. Note that the length of privacy screens will also be a multiple of 5, walks will be 5 feet wide, planting beds will be 5 feet across, and tree wells will be either 5 by 5 feet or 5 by 10 feet.

Slide Projector Planning

In addition to the sketches you're making over your base map, try using a slide projector to illustrate your ideas. It's a technique landscape architects and designers use to help clients visualize proposed designs or changes.

You'll need slides of the area you want to remodel, a projector, tracing paper, a soft pencil, and a fine- or medium-point felt-tip pen.

Set up the projector so it focuses on the screen or wall at a level where you can work sitting down. Tape a sheet of tracing paper over the projected image and begin by sketching in the proposed changes. (With features such as doors, windows, roof, and ground lines already in the slide, it should be easy for you to maintain correct scale and dimension.) Use as many sheets of paper as you need.

When you're satisfied with your design, use a dark felt-tip pen to draw in the permanent existing background. Don't worry about capturing every detail—your eye will compensate for features that you've suggested with just a few lines.

Laying the Proper Groundwork

Designing your patio isn't only a matter of planning its use areas and determining its structures and style. An integral part of the process is constant observance of the "lay of the land," specifically grading and drainage.

Grading. Whenever you can fit any landscape element into the existing topography with little or no disturbance of the soil, you'll save time, effort, and expense.

However, that isn't always possible. More often, the existing topography has inherent problems, or you'll decide to alter it in order to accommodate your ideal design. Then you must grade the land: reshape it by removing soil, filling in with soil, or both. (When you're ready to do the work, see pages 82–84 for specific techniques.)

Why grade, specifically? Aside from such practical considerations as ensuring good surface drainage, grading is often required for esthetic reasons. Perhaps an uneven area destined to become a barbecue area needs smoothing out. Or maybe you've opted for an Oriental-style garden that calls for the creation of interesting contours. Flat, open landscapes frequently cry out for vertical dimension: sculpting a berm near a patio will add that dimension, as well as create privacy and make your yard more attractive.

If your property lies on a slope so steep that, without skillful grading and terracing, it would remain unstable and useless, consider constructing one or a series of retaining walls. The safest way to build the wall is to place it at the bottom of a gentle slope, if space permits, and fill in behind it with soil. That way you won't disturb the stability of the soil. Otherwise, the hill can be held either with a single high wall or with a series of low retaining walls that form terraces. The drawing on the facing page shows all three techniques.

Who should do the job? If the grading is simple and you have the time and inclination to do the work, you can save money and have the satisfaction of having literally shaped the land you'll live with for years to come. But many special situations—for example, a high retaining wall—require that you obtain professional help. (Consult your local building department for the restrictions that apply in your area.)

If the soil surrounding existing trees is to be graded, call in a tree expert who understands how to grade without jeopardizing the trees' health. If a steep or unstable slope requires terracing, contact a landscape architect or soils engineer, someone who can foresee all the implications and who is familiar with legal requirements. In short, you should rely on the expertise of professionals for major grading, including the grading of any unstable area.

Drainage. At the same time that you're studying the land's grade, you'll also be looking at its drainage. Wherever drainage is a problem, note the area and the solution, if you can determine it, on your base map and final sketches. For information on specific methods for improving drainage, see pages 82–83.

If your landscape is nearly flat, it must have adequate surface drainage: a minimum slope of 1 inch per 8 feet of paved surface, or nearly 3 inches per 10 feet of unpaved ground. Steeper gradients are better for slow-draining, heavy soils.

Always route water away from the house, using one of the approaches shown on the facing page. Where property slopes toward the house, you'll probably have to shore it up with a retaining wall, slope the surfaces inward as shown, and direct runoff to a central drain. Rapid runoff from roofs and paved surfaces sometimes requires a special solution, such as drain tiles or a catch basin.

Steep slopes absorb far less rainwater than flat areas and may drain fast enough to cause erosion. To retard it, such slopes need terracing and, sometimes, special structures. Appropriate ground covers and other plantings can also be used to slow runoff.

Subsurface drainage, or percolation, is the downward penetration of soil by water; it's slow in clay soils, compacted surface soils, soils with mixed layers and interfaces, and soils overlying hardpan. Poor subsurface drainage is also a problem where the water table is close to the surface. Plastic drainpipes or dry wells offer solutions in many cases; a major problem calls for a sump pump.

On steep clay slopes most water runs off; nevertheless, retained water can cause mud slides. Get professional help to plan and install a drainage system for such hillsides.

Drawing Up Your Final Plan

Once you've decided exactly how you want to use your patio, what general types of structures will fulfill the needs of those areas, and what alterations of gradient are called for, you're ready to draw up a final plan. This rendering is the final result of the design process; use it for fine-tuning, for estimating materials, and when talking with landscaping professionals.

To create your plan, you'll need the same basic collection of tools you used to draw your base map (see pages 66–67). Most versions include a plan view and elevation, such as the one shown on page 74. (The plan view is the classic bird's-eye view of the layout; the elevation, a straight-on view, shows how the yard looks to a person standing in one spot,

Grading & Drainage . . . an Overview

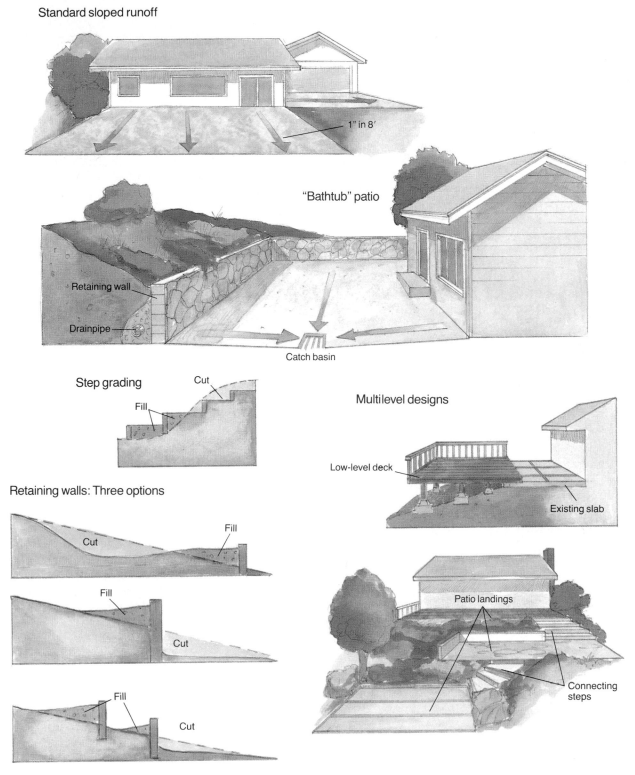

Standard sloped runoff

1" in 8'

"Bathtub" patio

Retaining wall

Drainpipe

Catch basin

Step grading

Cut

Fill

Multilevel designs

Low-level deck

Existing slab

Retaining walls: Three options

Fill

Cut

Fill

Cut

Fill

Cut

Patio landings

Connecting
steps

Uniform slope, shown at top, directs water away from house; hilly yards and retaining walls may require a central catch basin. Grading for steps and retaining walls requires cutting and filling (several options are shown at bottom left). A low-level deck and a series of detached patio landings are two solutions for hard-to-grade sites.

A Sample Final Plan

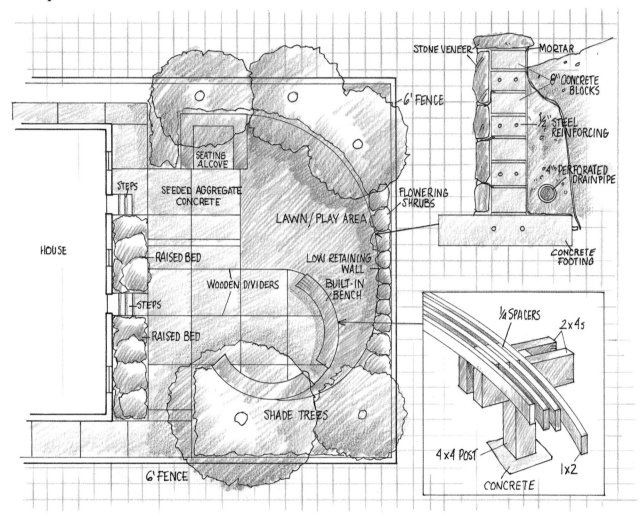

Labels within the plan drawing:

STONE VENEER — MORTAR — 8" CONCRETE BLOCKS — ½" STEEL REINFORCING — 4" PERFORATED DRAINPIPE — CONCRETE FOOTING

6' FENCE — SEATING ALCOVE — STEPS — SEEDED AGGREGATE CONCRETE — HOUSE — RAISED BED — STEPS — RAISED BED — WOODEN DIVIDERS — FLOWERING SHRUBS — LAWN / PLAY AREA — LOW RETAINING WALL — BUILT-IN BENCH — SHADE TREES — 6' FENCE

¼ SPACERS — 2x4s — 4x4 POST — 1x2 — CONCRETE

Sample final plan is end result of your design work. Main drawing, or plan view, is shown at left; an elevation (upper right) and detail (lower right) complete the picture.

looking in one direction.) Complex structures, such as spas, walls, or overheads, will probably call for additional details (see drawing above) or cross-sections (a slice through an object, rendered at an even larger scale).

Place a clean sheet of tracing paper directly over your base map. Label all features, as shown on the sample plan, trying to keep in mind what your plan will look like in three dimensions and in color. Make it as neat and concise as possible, and be sure your sketches and notations are bold enough to be read easily. (If you need copies of your final plan, a blueprinting company can make them quickly and inexpensively.)

If your final plan is too cluttered to read easily, if it calls for complicated structures, or if contractors will be relying on your plan for information on

construction, give your base map and final plan to a landscape architect or drafting professional for a final polishing.

Legal Considerations

Assigning your patio project to a landscape architect or contractor familiar with local building codes and zoning ordinances is one way to avoid worrying about them. If you're planning to do the work yourself, bring your plans to your local building department as soon as your ideas are reasonably solid.

Building codes. City and county building departments are charged with making sure that homes are structurally safe, free of health hazards, and within the legal rights of both homeowner and neighbors. Having reviewed thousands of home improvement plans over the years, building officials are well acquainted with the complications you may encounter, and they can be of valuable service to you.

Zoning ordinances. Zoning ordinances are designed mainly to keep commercial and residential properties separate, but in many jurisdictions these ordinances establish building setbacks from property lines as well as minimum height and maximum lot coverage requirements that could affect your plan.

Deed restrictions. In some communities—particularly where a certain architectural character prevails—you may find restrictions in your deed that limit the kind or extent of property improvements you can make. You may be limited to working in a particular style with certain materials (usually blending with the style of the house) or to building in specific locations on your lot.

Variances. If your proposed patio violates local zoning requirements, invades the required open space around the lot, or comes too close to the sidewalk, you can petition your local planning commission for a variance, which allows you to circumvent the restrictions. (Get the approval of your neighbors first; without it, your variance will probably be turned down.)

Building permits. Your patio project may not require a building permit; if it does, a single one may cover the job as a whole. If the project is complex, however, you may need a separate permit for wiring or plumbing. The fee for each permit is usually based on the value of the improvement.

Working with Professionals

Whatever your needs, professionals are available to help you out at every stage of the design and installation process. Even if you plan to do most of the work yourself, you may want to call in professionals for specific tasks, such as evaluating and polishing your final plans, or designing a particular structure. Or you may feel confident about your plans, but need help carrying them out.

Landscape architects. Landscape architects hold one or more degrees in their field and are trained (and in many states, licensed) to design both commercial and residential landscapes. Many are willing to give a simple consultation, either in their office or at your home, for a modest fee. They often can recommend a contractor to do the work.

Site Restrictions

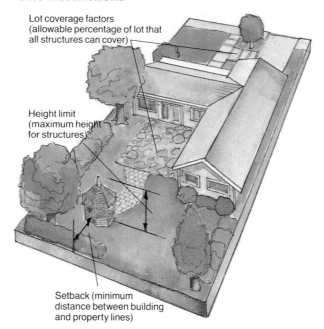

Lot coverage factors (allowable percentage of lot that all structures can cover)

Height limit (maximum height for structures)

Setback (minimum distance between building and property lines)

Local zoning ordinances may regulate setback, height of structures, and total lot coverage.

Landscape designers. Usually, landscape designers limit themselves to residential landscape design. They are unlicensed and meet no specific educational requirements, though many are extremely skilled and experienced.

Structural and soils engineers. These professionals need to be consulted if you're planning to build a structure on an unstable or steep lot, or where heavy wind or loads come into play.

Soils engineers evaluate soil conditions and establish design specifications for foundations; structural engineers, often working with the calculations a soils engineer provides, design foundation piers and footings to suit the site.

Landscape contractors. These professionals are trained (and in some states, licensed) to install landscapes: plantings, pavings, structures, and irrigation systems. Some also offer design services, which may be included in the total price of materials and installation.

Subcontractors. You may prefer to act as your own general contractor, hiring and supervising the skilled workers for your project. Subcontractors can usually supply you with current product information, sell fixtures and supplies, and do work according to the specifications of technical drawings and the standards of local codes.

DESIGNS FOR A SMALL LOT

Suppose you have a flat, rectangular backyard that's nondescript and very small. That's the challenge we presented to four landscape architects, each from a different locale, when we asked them to come up with a design for the yard. Our idea was not to illustrate a single "best" solution to a problem, but to show that, for any situation, there are likely to be a number of successful treatments. (For a look at a larger lot, see pages 78–79.)

In addition to giving the landscape architects a thumbnail sketch of the yard (shown at right), we presented them with some "conditions" about the site and the owners. We described the owners as professionals in their early forties with two teenagers and no pets. The owners, we said, do not wish to make any structural changes to the house, but want a relaxing, beautiful retreat with plants that are in keeping with their climate and water resources.

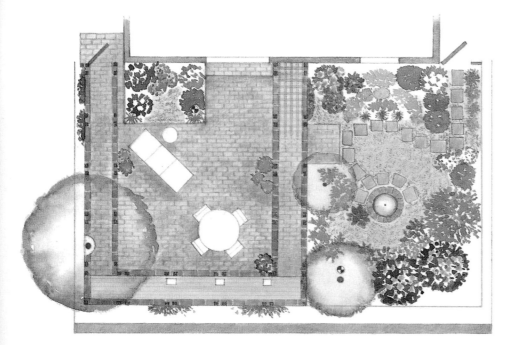

New England Appeal

An expansive light red brick patio off the family room looks right at home in this New England design; header courses of darker bricks echo the line of the lattice trellis enclosure. Azaleas and hydrangeas on one side of the door and a kitchen herb garden on the other add color.

On the garden side, stepping-stones lead to a small stone pool and fountain. Two rhododendrons, a vernal witch hazel, and a kousa dogwood hide the shed; a sour gum tree anchors the opposite (southwest) corner. A bench with built-in uplights is tucked below the trellis along the back wall. Landscape architect: Carol R. Johnson & Associates, Inc., Cambridge, Massachusetts.

Indoor/Outdoor Space

This Florida design links the indoors with the outside and creates a soothing, private environment with lush but low-maintenance landscaping.

The multipurpose patio is paved with concrete keystone, a locally manufactured product. The focal point, a black olive tree, provides essential afternoon shade. Another tree shields the view of the neighbor's deck; tall wild plantain screens out the shed.

The gunite goldfish pond's burbling waterfall soothes eyes and ears. Water lilies float on the surface; keystone stepping-stones cross the pond. The new eastern wall is tiled with mirrors to expand the space. The other walls are planted with a variety of creeping fig, a close-growing vine. Landscape architect: A. Gail Boorman & Associates, Naples, Florida.

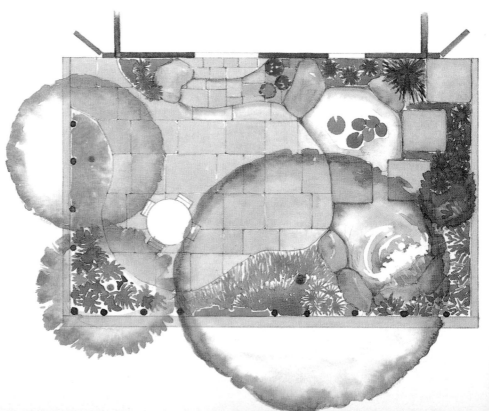

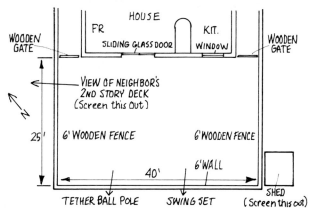

Here's a sketch of the lot we gave to the four landscape architects. Not only is it flat and empty, but there are no special features or plants on the neighboring properties worth including visually. However, there are some undesirable features: a second-story deck on the house next door, a shed abutting the back corner of the property, wood side fences that are in poor condition, and a neighbor's swing set and tetherball pole that are visible above an unattractive back wall.

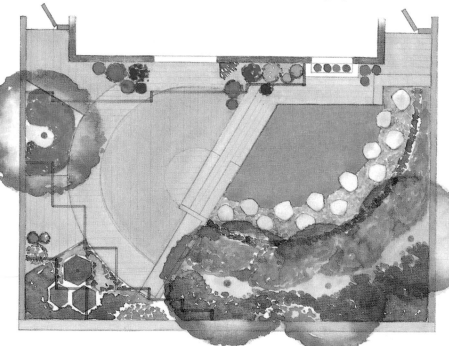

Northwest Cedar Deck

The availability of wood in the Pacific Northwest and the popularity of the outdoors result in this low-level deck solution. New French doors flanked by colorful pots open to the decking, 2 by 4s laid on edge in a fanlike pattern. Steps stretch out as patio seating. A pop-out window off the kitchen is filled with herbs; below is a garden storage area.

A stepping-stone pathway, with river rock in between, skirts the moss garden, which functions like grass but needs no mowing. Three vine maples hide the shed, a fourth screens off the neighbors' deck. A fountain in the southwest corner has three basalt columns, with the lowest drilled for a recirculating bubbler. A vine-covered trellis provides enclosure. Landscape architect: Harvard & Associates, Seattle, Washington.

The California Solution

Local flagstone paving, natural boulders, and waterwise plantings distinguish this design from Southern California.

Cut stone pavers set 18 inches below floor level are reached by a poured concrete landing and steps softened by a large planter. In the south corner, the pavers give way to an angular garden pool with waterfall. Native boulders retain planting beds.

Privacy is ensured by new stucco walls clad with trumpet vine; by a two-story, bougainvillea-covered trellis that screens the eastern view; and by Leyland cypress trees that block both the shed and the neighbors' second-story deck. Landscape architect: Eriksson, Peters, Thoms, San Juan Capistrano, California.

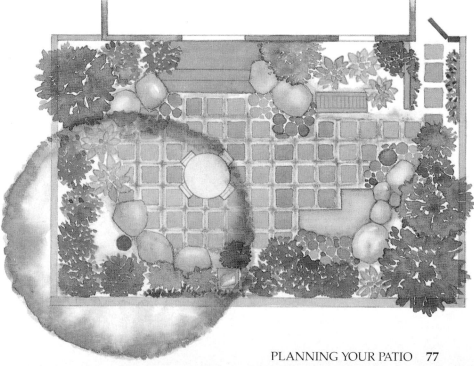

DESIGNS FOR A LARGE LOT

As we did with the small lot shown on pages 76–77, we asked a group of landscape architects from different areas to give our large lot (shown at right) a new life.

The lot we presented to the landscape professionals this time is larger, with room for some amenities and with a sloping grade that opens up a number of options. It's now empty except for a tree and a small concrete slab, neither of which the owners are particularly attached to. A door from the living room leads out to the existing patio. The bedrooms, which are several feet above grade in this split-level house, offer a view of the yard.

Again, we described the homeowners as professionals with two teenage children. They enjoy outdoor entertaining, but would also like space for private relaxation, and are willing to make small structural changes to realize their goals. The owners want to screen out the view of their neighbors' backyard on one side of their property. Although they possess no special skills, they would like to be able to do some of the work themselves.

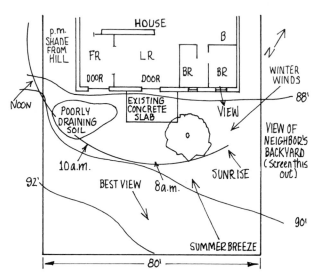

The large yard, which is bare except for a concrete slab and a tree, falls several feet to the house. Doors from both the family room and living room lead outside.

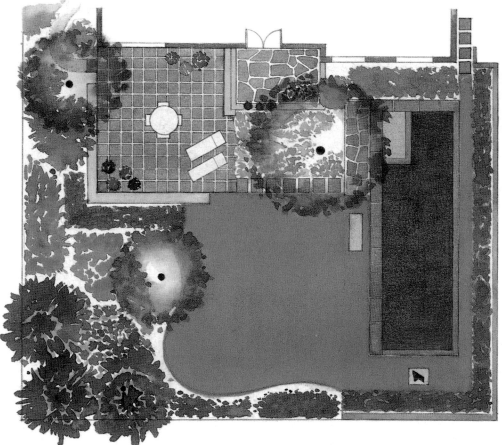

Neat & Orderly

This formal and precise East Coast plan features bluestone pavement in two patterns: an irregular but highly crafted version off the kitchen and a 2-foot cut pattern for the main patio area.

The large, elegant lawn and 12-by 40-foot lap pool with integral spa are major entertainment areas; here, the lot has been graded flat, and drainage for runoff is provided. The dark lap pool reflects the sky; the sculpture at the end of the pool is an important focal point and can be viewed from the bedrooms.

The hillside garden in the south corner, visible from the house and patio, provides texture and color, as does the perennial garden in the corner of the patio. The high evergreen hedge both screens the adjacent property and establishes a calm and visually protected environment. Stone walls set off the geometric hardscape from the softer plantings. Landscape architect: Stephenson & Good, Washington, D.C.

Many Spaces in One

This multispace, multilevel solution artfully combines a variety of materials and use areas. The principal patio surface is flagstone, accessed from the house by sliding glass doors. Beyond is an expanse of lawn, a possible future pool site, along with a private sitting alcove fitted with a built-in bench and partially shaded by tall trees. Flagstones laid in sand provide the paving underfoot.

Opposite, steps climb up to a wood deck equipped with a barbecue, a tiled serving counter, and built-in seating. The deck opens at the back to a boulder-edged natural pool and small waterfall. Behind is a second, more private deck, complete with a spa and an arbor with built-in towel racks and lights.

Drought-tolerant plantings line the fences and property lines; thirstier plants are adjacent to the house. Landscape architect: Ransohoff, Blanchfield, Jones, Inc., Redwood City, California.

Native Scene

Native plantings are at the heart of this backyard makeover: California live oaks form the backdrop and shield the view in the rear of the yard; twin bay trees, a tababuia, and the existing tree, a sycamore, add their shade. Other native grasses, wildflowers, and shrubs fill in the understory.

The lot is divided into a number of mini-patios: the one off the living area is paved with Bouquet Canyon stone (a local variety) set on concrete; a small elevated patio outside the bedrooms (one of which has been fitted with doors) has two sets of stairs, one planted with grass. The lap pool is bordered by stone walls that negotiate the ascending slope. Beyond is a stone-edged spa, another stone wall, and a winding path of decomposed granite that leads to a private wood-and-shingle pavilion.

A formal rose garden on one side of the yard and a small vegetable garden off the family room complete the design. Landscape architect: Katzmaier Newell Kehr, Corona Del Mar, California.

BUILDING
TECHNIQUES

This chapter sets out the procedures you'll need to follow in order to build your patio. It begins with information on preparing the site and laying edgings, two prerequisites to a successful patio project. We then present construction methods for the basic patio materials—brick, concrete, pavers, ceramic tile, adobe, stone, wood, and loose materials. In addition, the construction of such complementary structural elements as retaining walls, raised beds, and steps is explained. The chapter ends with a handy reference section on maintaining and repairing your patio surface.

Woven throughout the chapter are special features addressing the installation of such amenities as benches and planters, as well as a section on dismantling an existing concrete or asphalt patio.

As with any building project, always check with your building department about code restrictions that may apply to your project. Also, be sure to take into account soil, drainage, and frost conditions in your area. Local officials and landscape professionals can be a real help here.

Easy-to-solve Jigsaw Puzzle

Interlocking concrete pavers are simple to lay: start with a level, screeded bed of damp sand, place pavers carefully, then snug them down with a mallet and check level. For complete installation details, see pages 112–113.

SITE PREPARATION

Regardless of the paving you choose, you will, in most cases, have to prepare a foundation or sub-base. This is probably the single most important step in your entire patio project. The foundation affects not only your patio's life span but also its finished appearance. Since the base you lay will depend on your paving material, be sure to consult the section on that particular material for specific requirements.

Most properties need just minor leveling; some may also require a short retaining wall (see pages 132–133). However, the grading of some sites—low-lying areas, steep slopes and hillsides, and areas with unstable soil, for example—can pose serious problems. In these cases, it's best to consult a landscape architect or landscape contractor.

Note: Be on the lookout for underground water, gas, or electrical lines running through your patio site. These systems, plus lawn sprinklers or existing drains, may need rerouting before you can proceed.

Drainage

Whenever you pave an area, its drainage is affected, since water tends to run off even the most porous paving. Unless the area to be paved slopes naturally, it must be graded before paving so that runoff won't collect where it will cause problems—against a house foundation, for example. You should provide a pitch of at least 1 inch in 8 feet (or 1/8 inch per foot).

Often, the bed you lay below the paving, whether it's sand or a thicker layer of gravel, will provide adequate drainage. But sometimes, additional provisions are necessary.

Perforated drainpipe. To draw off most of the water that collects under the paving, you can place perforated plastic drainpipe in a narrow trench

dug under the center or around the edge of the paved area.

Dig the trench about 12 inches deep (deeper where the ground freezes) and lay the pipe, perforated side down, in the trench. Pack in gravel to a depth of 6 inches and replace the soil. If the trench is under the patio site, keep the fill soaked for a few days to ensure that it's properly packed.

To route a drainage trench through a mortared patio, first pour a concrete channel, as shown below; then leave open (ungrouted) joints between units bridging the trench.

Catch basin. To drain water from a low-lying area, use a catch basin, digging the hole for it at the lowest point. Either set a ready-made concrete catch basin (available at building supply stores) into the hole or form and pour the concrete base and sides yourself (for help, see pages 100–107).

Set a grate on top and dig a trench from the hole for a drainpipe to direct accumulated water toward a disposal place, such as a dry well, storm drain (if allowed), or gentle slope. Avoid sending the runoff toward areas already boggy when it rains; it will only make the problem worse.

Drainage Examples

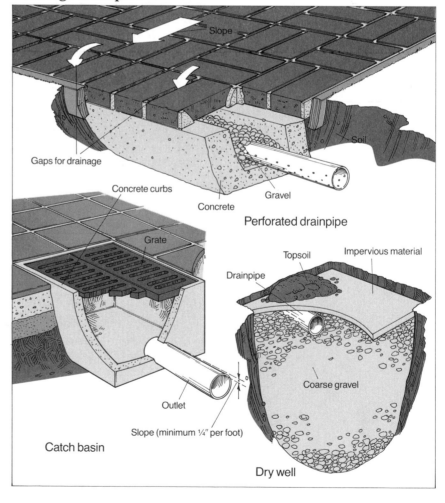

Slope

Gaps for drainage

Concrete curbs

Soil

Gravel

Concrete

Perforated drainpipe

Grate

Impervious material

Topsoil

Drainpipe

Outlet

Slope (minimum 1/4" per foot)

Coarse gravel

Catch basin

Dry well

You'll also need a catch basin and a drain for a patio enclosed by retaining walls; such a setup creates a "bathtub" effect. Slope the patio at all points toward the outlet.

Dry well. To build a dry well, dig a 2- to 4-foot-wide hole at least 3 feet deep (keep the bottom above the water table). Next, dig trenches for the drainpipes that will carry water into the dry well from other areas. Fill the dry well with coarse gravel or small rocks, and cover it with an impervious material, such as heavy roofing paper. Conceal it with topsoil.

Final Grading

Once you've determined where to send the runoff, you're ready to start grading. Usually, this means you'll be digging out the area to be paved. Try to avoid filling and tamping; tamped earth is never as firm as undisturbed soil, and it will inevitably settle, taking your paving with it.

Basic layout. Here's the procedure for laying out a typical rectangular patio adjacent to a house. For an illustration, see the drawing below.

First determine the preferred level for the finished surface. Next, mark off the patio's location with batterboards; drive them in at the corners of the area you're paving, placing them at least a foot, but not more than 4 feet, back from the patio's perimeter.

Drive a nail into the house where the corner of the patio will meet it. (For masonry sidings, drive the nail into a stake.) Attach mason's twine to the nail and stretch it out to the batterboard on that side.

To check the corner for square, measure back 3 feet along the house and make a mark. Make a second mark 4 feet along the taut twine. When the distance between the two points measures exactly 5 feet, the twine is at a right angle to the house. Wrap the line tightly around the batterboard. (This triangulation method works in any multiple of 3-4-5—for instance, 6-8-10 or 9-12-15. For maximum accuracy, use the largest ratio possible.)

Repeat this procedure on the other side. Then measure out the exact distance along each of these side lines, mark the twines, and attach a "back" line to the batterboards.

To double-check your work, measure the distance between opposite corners and adjust the lines until the diagonals are equal. Your patio outline should now be square.

Drive stakes into the ground both at the corners of the patio adjacent to the house and at the outside corners, as shown. Mark the desired patio level on the stakes adjacent to the house. Attach a twine to each house stake, stretch it toward the outside stake, and level it with a line level placed at the center of the span. Mark each corner stake where the twine crosses it.

To allow for the standard pitch (1 inch in 8 feet), figure your total drop and mark this on each corner stake below the level mark. Restring the perimeter lines at this level, attaching them to new outside stakes.

(Continued on next page)

Laying Out Lines

Careful layout is the key to a first-rate patio installation. Batterboards and mason's lines define perimeter; triangulation method and diagonal measurements (left inset) help ensure square. Mark stakes for total drop (right inset).

Digging the Foundation

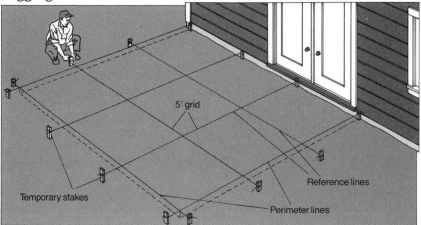

Before beginning any grading, install a gridwork of temporary stakes and lines intersecting perimeter lines; pull reference lines tight.

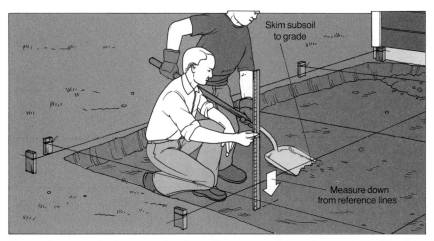

Excavate as required, measuring down from your gridwork repeatedly. By skimming subsoil carefully at a shallow angle, you'll disturb less soil.

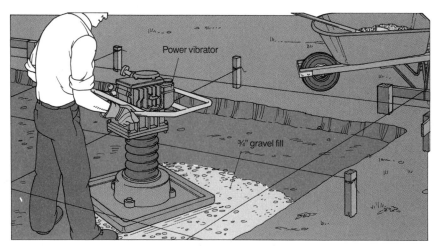

Fill any low areas with decomposed granite; put down a little bit at a time, wet it down, and tamp, either with a power vibrator or by hand. Build up additional layers as needed.

Irregular patio shapes call for additional stakes and lines—use the 3-4-5 method to ensure squareness.

To lay out an arc or circle, use a long board or straightedge. Stake or nail it to the ground at the center of the arc, measure off the radius, and pivot the board; mark the arc with builder's chalk or lime.

Lay out freeform curves with a garden hose or rope, and check from all angles. Then stake the rope or hose in place.

Plan to leave a gap—½ inch or greater—where the patio surface meets a house or another structure. Galvanized metal flashing protects wood siding or floor framing from moisture damage. An expansion strip (see page 102) is another option; attach it ½ inch below finished paving height. Seal it later with a waterproof caulking compound.

Excavation. Working off your established perimeter, add more lines and stakes in 5-foot squares to use as a reference while digging, as shown above. Next, remove the sod (if you're on grass), working several inches past your perimeter lines so you have room to install edgings. You can use either a sharp spade or a rented sod cutter to cut the sod into manageable strips.

Using a square-sided shovel and measuring down from the lines, excavate below them a distance equal to the paving thickness plus the thickness of the setting bed. The trick is to "skim" along parallel to the ground, removing the minimum amount of soil required to reach the correct depth. Avoid disturbing soil unnecessarily. (The excavation doesn't have to be perfect—the setting bed will correct small irregularities—but it pays to use extra care at this point.)

If you must even out a low spot, use decomposed granite, spreading it evenly with a rake; moisten it, then tamp it several times with a hand tamper or a rented power vibrator.

EDGINGS

Whether you lay it, hammer it, set it, or pour it in place, a patio or walkway will almost always require an edging. In addition to outlining the surface, edgings confine the surfacing material within a desired area, an important function when you're using loose materials, pouring concrete, or setting bricks in sand. Most often, edgings are made of wood, but masonry can also be utilized effectively.

When used to curb paved areas, edgings are usually installed after the base has been prepared (see pages 82–84) and before the setting bed and paving are laid. Before you begin work, make sure you're familiar with the construction sequence for the paving you're laying.

Wood Edgings

To build wood edgings, choose a wood that's highly resistant to rot and termites, such as pressure-treated lumber or the heartwood of cedar, redwood, or certain types of cypress.

Dimension-lumber edgings. The most popular edgings are made of 2 by 4 or 2 by 6 lumber, but, for special emphasis, you can also use 4 by 4 or 6 by 6 material. The installation sequence is shown at right.

The mason's twine you strung around the perimeter of the area to be paved during grading marks the exact outside top edge of the edgings. To achieve the correct finished height, you'll probably have to to dig narrow trenches under the lines.

Cut the boards to the correct lengths; then join one or more corners together, using drywall screws or galvanized box nails. Drive several 12-inch stakes (1 by 3s or 2 by 2s) into the soil, aligning their inner faces with the twine.

Position the edging boards against the inside faces of the stakes, level with the twine, and fasten the stakes

to the boards. Go back and place additional stakes no more than 4 feet apart; where edging boards are butted, either add doubled stakes or splice the boards.

Cut off the stake tops so they angle up to the top of the edging boards. Pack soil tightly around the outer perimeter.

Other wood edgings. Heavy timbers and railroad ties make strong, showy edgings and interior dividers,

especially when drilled and threaded with steel pipe (see illustration on page 86).

In addition to rustic timbers, you can use wood posts or logs, in diameters ranging from 2 to 6 inches, to form a series of miniature pilings. Set them vertically, butted tightly against one another; the bottoms should rest in concrete, not in bare ground. Pack soil around the pilings. For a more finished look, top off 4 by 4s with a horizontal 2 by 4 or 2 by 6 cap.

(Continued on next page)

Installing Wood Edgings

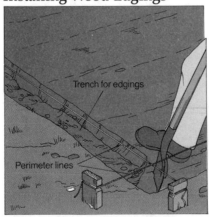

Standard wood edgings may require a narrow trench; dig below perimeter lines as shown.

Drive in 1 by 3 or 2 by 2 stakes flush with perimeter lines, using a small sledgehammer.

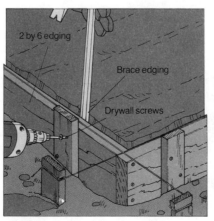

After fastening edging boards together, position them against stakes; fasten stakes to edgings as shown.

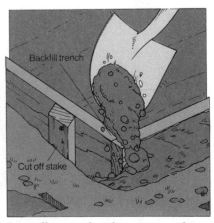

Saw off exposed stakes at an angle below tops of edgings; then pack excavated soil around the outside.

Curved wood edgings. If your patio design calls for gentle curves, use flexible redwood benderboard.

First, dig a trench as for dimension-lumber edging. Soak the benderboard in water to make it more flexible. Then bend it around guide stakes set on the inside edge of the curve and nail or screw the board to the stakes (see drawing below). For an outside curve, add stakes every 3 feet or so on the outside and fasten the benderboard to them; then pull up the inside stakes.

Bend additional boards around the first board, staggering any splices, until you've built up the curved edging to the same thickness as the straight sections. Nail all layers together between stakes with 2d (1-inch) nails.

Brick Edgings

The easiest masonry edgings to build are brick-in-soil edgings. Be sure to check soil conditions first, however; only very firm soil will hold the bricks in place without adding mortar. "Invisible" edgings (see at right) are stronger and are particularly effective with brick-in-sand paving; they're adaptable to other masonry units as well.

Brick-in-soil edgings. In the drawing below, bottom right, the soil has been cut away to show a row of "soldiers"—bricks standing side by side. You can set the bricks vertically, horizontally, or, for a sawtooth effect, at a uniform angle.

To install brick-in-soil edgings, first grade the area to be paved (see pages 83–84). Dig a narrow trench around the perimeter deep enough so that the tops of the soldiers will be flush with the finished paving. Then position the soldiers, leveling their tops as you work. Pack soil against the outside.

Invisible edgings. An invisible edging is actually a small, underground concrete footing that secures paving units without any visible support. Paving units set into the surface of the concrete conceal the footing.

If you're using brick-in-sand paving, build temporary forms around the patio perimeter as for a concrete footing. Make the forms one brick-length wide in a trench deep enough

More Edging Options

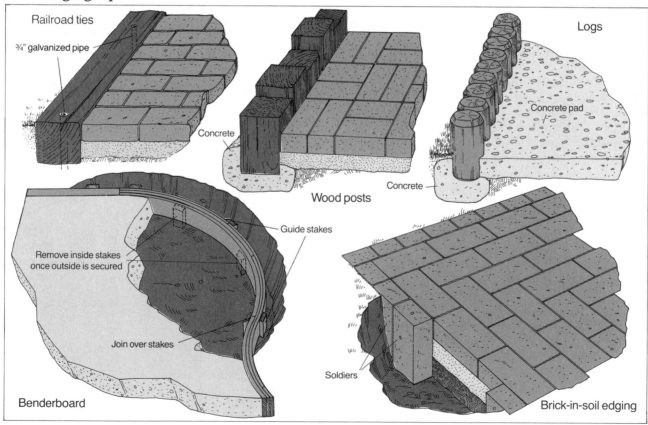

Railroad ties

¾" galvanized pipe

Concrete

Logs

Concrete pad

Concrete

Wood posts

Guide stakes

Remove inside stakes once outside is secured

Join over stakes

Benderboard

Soldiers

Brick-in-soil edging

to allow for a 4-inch-deep concrete bed (deeper where the ground freezes). The forms should be at finished paving height.

Pour in concrete and, using a bladed screed, level it one brick thick below the top of the forms, as shown below. Place edging bricks in the wet concrete, butting their joints, and set them with a rubber mallet. Let the concrete cure (see pages 106–107) before packing soil around it.

Stone Edgings

A rustic or woodsy landscape may provide a good setting for edgings made of cut flagstone or a more informal edging of rocks and boulders.

Flagstone. Before laying flagstone or other small stones, arrange them in a pleasing pattern, cutting them where necessary. Then lay the stones in 1-inch-thick mortar (see pages 121–122).

Uncut stone. Usually, larger rocks and boulders look best if they're partially buried; otherwise, prop them up with smaller rocks and then pack the area with soil and plantings. Irregularly shaped stones blend well with loose materials. Cut formal paving units to fit around the boulders.

Plastic Edgings

Manufactured plastic edgings are an easy-to-install option for do-it-your-

selfers. The strips secure bricks or concrete pavers below finished paving height. You can conceal the strips with soil or sod. Flexible sections negotiate tight curves; rigid strips can also follow curves if kerfed. Secure plastic edgings with oversize (10- to 12-inch) spikes.

Concrete Edgings

Concrete edgings are built similarly to invisible edgings. Build forms, pour concrete, and then screed it flush with the top of the forms so that the edging will be even with the paved surface. Finish the concrete as desired (for some ideas, turn to pages 107–109) and let it cure.

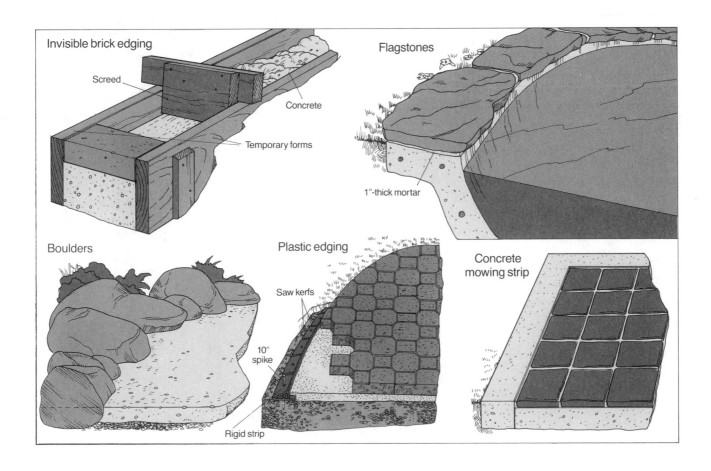

Invisible brick edging
Screed
Concrete
Temporary forms

Flagstones
1"-thick mortar

Boulders

Plastic edging
Saw kerfs
10" spike
Rigid strip

Concrete mowing strip

DEMOLISHING YOUR OWN CONCRETE OR ASPHALT PAVING

When you need to remove a concrete or asphalt patio or driveway, the equipment shown here will get the job done. Just be sure you're ready for a vigorous workout: tearing up paving requires lots of elbow grease.

If you're doing the work yourself, it helps to be familiar with the basic tools used for concrete and asphalt demolition: hand tools such as pikes, sledgehammers, and crowbars; pneumatic and electric jackhammers; and concrete saws. You can rent those tools you don't have; just be sure each tool is thoroughly checked for safety.

If you'd rather have a professional do the work, look for contractors in the Yellow Pages under "Concrete Breaking, Cutting, and Sawing." Jackhammer work is priced by the square foot; sometimes, the cost of hauling away the rubble is included. Typically, contractors charge by the linear foot for asphalt and concrete sawing.

Wearing shatterproof goggles or safety glasses is an absolute must when you work with tools that produce flying chips. It's also wise to wear leather gloves, heavy long pants, sturdy shoes, and hearing protectors or earplugs.

Sledgehammers & Crowbars

Wielded by strong arms, a sledgehammer or a 4- or 5-foot crowbar works surprisingly fast, depending on the thickness of the paving to be removed.

A large pike will perform extremely well on 3-inch-thick asphalt on a cool day: you should be able to pry up 1-foot-square sections nearly as fast as with a small jackhammer. On hot days, it's a different story, however. Warmed to the consistency of tar, asphalt bends when it's pried, comes loose in tiny chunks, and sticks to clothes and tools.

Jackhammers

Pneumatic jackhammers, the heavyweights of concrete demolition, operate on air supplied by a compressor, which is run by a gasoline or diesel engine. The compressed air is delivered to the jackhammer through a heavy-duty hose.

Jackhammer units are usually rented on a trailer that you tow behind your car. Many rental outfits offer a choice of sizes—jackhammers that operate with 30, 60, or 90 cubic feet of air per minute (cfm). Each jackhammer weighs approximately the same number of pounds as its cfm rating.

The lightest model, the 30-pounder, is best used for breaking asphalt or concrete 2 to 3 inches thick. Sixty-pound jackhammers handle concrete up to 4 inches thick—the depth of most patios and drive-

Demolition Tools

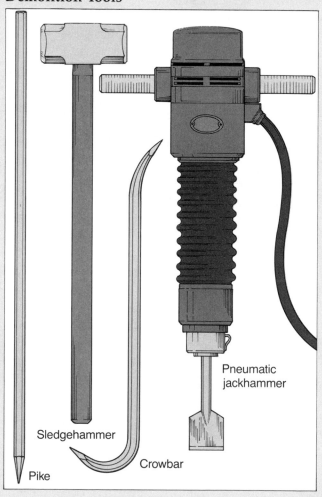

Pike

Sledgehammer

Crowbar

Pneumatic jackhammer

ways. Ninety-pound jackhammers can break through concrete up to 12 inches thick (foundations, for example), but they wear you out in the process.

Electric jackhammers are smaller, lighter in weight, and quieter than pneumatic ones. They're also less powerful, running on 110-volt household current. Use them on small areas of relatively thin (3 inches or less) concrete or asphalt.

Several different kinds of points (also called steels) used for various jackhammering jobs are shown below. Take care when changing or removing steel points: points heated by friction can burn an ungloved hand.

When you're operating a jackhammer, let the machine do the work. If you lean on the tool, you'll be in for a bone-jarring ride. Use your hands and

arms only to balance the tool. It's easiest to break off the concrete in small, 3- to 5-inch-wide chunks.

If the point gets completely embedded with no sign of the concrete cracking, pull it out immediately and move closer to the broken edge. Otherwise, you risk embedding the point so tightly that getting it out could be difficult.

Concrete Saws for Straight Cuts

To remove only a strip of concrete, leaving the rest intact with a finished edge, you'll need to rent a concrete saw. With the proper blade, you can also use it to cut asphalt.

A concrete saw moves on three or four wheels as it cuts. A gasoline engine drives the saw blade; when the clutch is engaged, the engine also propels the saw forward.

If a finished edge is not too important, make a scoring cut about ½ inch deep. Then hit the concrete beyond the cut with a sledge or jackhammer; the concrete will break off cleanly, but the edge will be a bit irregular below the cut.

Where a finished edge is important, lower the blade the full depth of the concrete (you raise and lower the blade by means of a manually operated gear). As you would expect, it's faster to make a scoring cut than a full-depth one.

Two kinds of circular blades are commonly available: carborundum and diamond-edged. If you want the carborundum blade, you'll probably have to buy it. Diamond blades usually rent for $20 to $30 a day, with an additional charge for blade wear, but if you plan to cut more than 40 linear feet of concrete, renting a diamond-edged blade may be less expensive than buying all the carborundum ones you'll need.

Diamond blades must be cooled by water; with carborundum types, water helps extend the blade's cutting life. On one side of your concrete saw, you'll find a place to connect the garden hose; turn on the water before you start the machine.

Start the motor and position the blade over the line. Lower the blade very slowly through the concrete; if you force it, you risk breaking the blade or snapping off a diamond-edged saw tooth. Push the saw forward as required.

Concrete saws are extremely difficult to use on even a moderately sloping surface. Consider hiring a professional if you plan to cut on more than about a 3° slope.

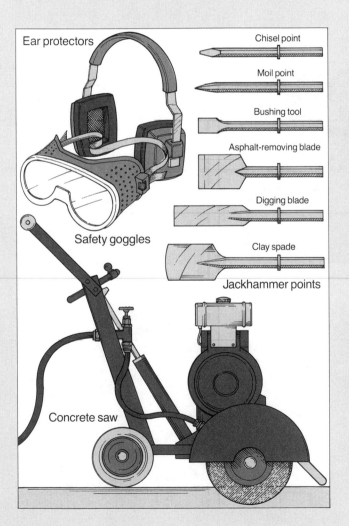

Ear protectors

Chisel point

Moil point

Bushing tool

Asphalt-removing blade

Safety goggles

Digging blade

Clay spade

Jackhammer points

Concrete saw

BRICK

Building with brick is pleasant work. The units are sized for easy one-hand lifting, and bricklaying takes on a certain rhythm once you get the hang of it. Even the tools and techniques you'll need are basic.

As discussed on pages 12–15, you have many options in brick types, textures, and colors. Patio patterns can be as creative as your imagination—and your brick-cutting skills—dictate.

Brick paving methods include brick-in-sand, dry mortar, and wet mortar. The first is the easiest technique for beginners; dry mortar is a variation on the brick-in-sand method. The wet mortar method, which produces the most formal re-sults, is best done by experienced bricklayers only.

Shopping for Materials

You can find most brick types at masonry suppliers or building and landscape supply yards; look in the Yellow Pages under "Brick" or "Building Materials." For secondhand brick and used companion materials, such as cobbles and wood timbers, salvage yards are often good sources.

When you order, ask about delivery charges. Though they're usually low, they're often not included in the quoted price. Paying a little more to have the bricks delivered on a pallet prevents the considerable breakage that can result when the bricks are merely dumped off a truck.

Make sure your dealer has enough of the bricks you need to complete your project. If you have to use a different variety or some bricks from another supplier, you may not be able to complete the pattern you've started.

When you're laying bricks with the wet mortar method, you'll need mortar. Mortar recipes vary according to their intended use, but the ingredients are always the same: cement, hydrated lime, sand, and water.

If your job is small, ready-mix mortar, available by the bag at build-

Basic Brick Patterns

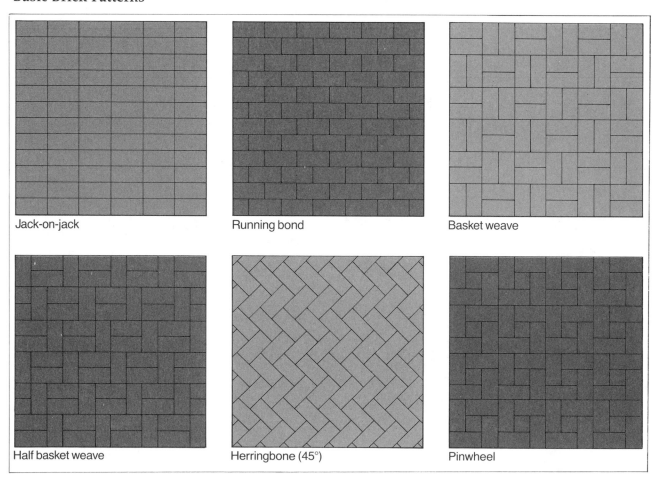

Jack-on-jack

Running bond

Basket weave

Half basket weave

Herringbone (45°)

Pinwheel

ing supply stores, is your best bet. Ask your building supplier if the recipe is the right one for your project.

Patio Patterns

When choosing a brick pattern (also known as the bond), keep in mind the degree of difficulty involved. Some bonds demand not only accuracy but also a lot of cutting of bricks. The patterns shown are some of the most popular; jack-on-jack and running bond are the two simplest to lay.

Your choice of bond will also be affected by whether you plan to lay the bricks with closed joints (butted together) or open joints (spaced).

Variations in the sizes of common clay brick make some patterns difficult to complete when the bricks are tightly butted. A pattern like jack-on-jack, for example, is hard to maintain over a large area. When laid solid, basket weave will produce a curious effect: a ½-inch hole turns up in the center of each block of eight bricks.

If you're using a common brick that varies in size, open joints give you the flexibility to take up the differences in size. Where closed joints are required, consider more uniform paver bricks (look for "true" or "mortarless" pavers).

When you pave a large area in a single bond, the surface can become monotonous. To avoid this problem, try changing the direction of the bond to add variety. Another solution is to combine two patterns. For example, you can break up a large surface of diagonal herringbone by dissecting it with a few rows of jack-on-jack. Or add a double row of running bond to a basket weave pattern.

Mixing brick colors—alternating light and dark within simple patterns, mixing colors and patterns, or concentrating on a special border treatment—also adds design interest.

Another effective touch is to introduce a different building material,

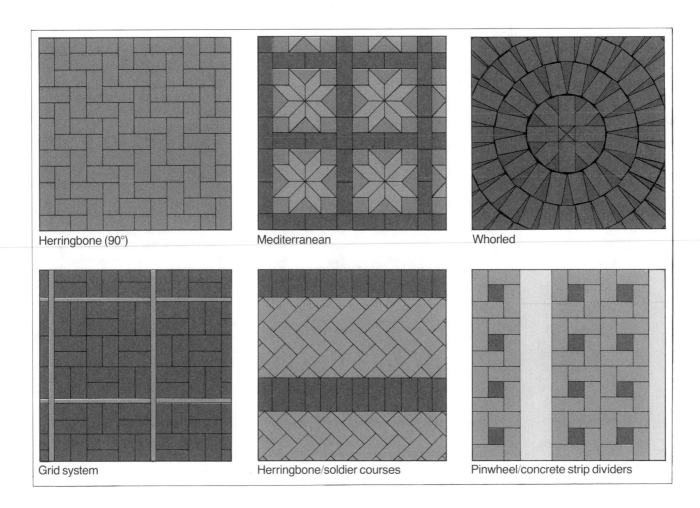

Herringbone (90°)

Mediterranean

Whorled

Grid system

Herringbone/soldier courses

Pinwheel/concrete strip dividers

Bricklaying Tools

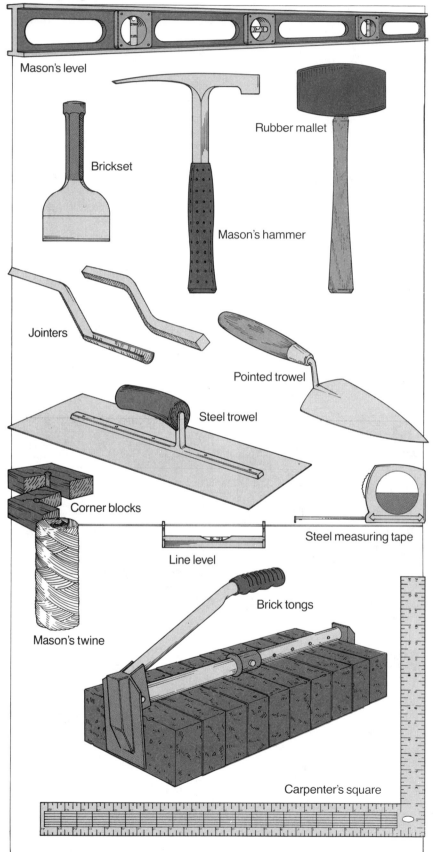

Mason's level

Brickset

Rubber mallet

Mason's hammer

Jointers

Pointed trowel

Steel trowel

Corner blocks

Steel measuring tape

Mason's twine

Line level

Brick tongs

Carpenter's square

such as wood or concrete. You can break up a basket weave pattern with a grid system of redwood or cedar (the building technique is the same as for wood edgings; see page 85). The same grid-system idea can be created with strips of concrete. Railroad ties are also popular.

Before you build, lay out your design on graph paper, making allowance for joints as desired. You may even want to buy a few brick samples to try out at home. Or you can cut out cardboard shapes and arrange them on the ground. Don't be afraid to use your imagination—but take care not to make the pattern too busy, especially if you're paving a small area.

Bricklaying Tools & Techniques

A quick search of your toolshed or workshop will usually turn up a number of the tools you'll need: a 2-foot carpenter's level, a carpenter's square, a steel measuring tape, and a rubber mallet.

Specialized tools. Some additional tools (shown at left) will make the job go more smoothly. Mason's twine is good for laying out perimeter lines or guides for straight courses; corner blocks hold the line in place. A small line level allows you to fine-tune long perimeter lines. A mason's level at least 4 feet long is helpful for checking level over a large area.

A brickset or a broad-bladed cold chisel is handy for cutting and dressing bricks. For most jobs involving mortar, you'll need a pointed trowel with a 10-inch blade.

Optional equipment includes jointers to shape mortar joints, a mason's hammer to chip away rough edges of a cut brick, a steel trowel, and brick tongs. A wheelbarrow, a square-sided shovel, and a hand tamper may also come in handy.

Cutting brick. No matter how carefully you plan, some brick cutting is almost inevitable, especially when you're setting a bond where the bricks overlap, such as running bond or diagonal herringbone. Save all your cutting for last so you can do it all at once when you're certain of exact sizes and shapes.

If you have just a few cuts to make, the best tool is the brickset. Set the brick on flat sand and place the chisel (with the bevel facing away from the piece to be used) along the cut line (see drawing at right). To cut the brick, tap the chisel sharply with a heavy, soft-headed steel hammer (wear safety goggles). For cleaner results, tap the brick lightly to score a groove across all four sides before the final blow. If necessary, chip away the rough edges with the brickset or a mason's hammer.

If you have a lot of cutting to do, you can rent a hydraulic brick cutter, a large, stationary tool that scores and then snaps a brick under pressure. The results are fairly clean, but, as with a brickset, you'll probably want to dress the cut. If repeated angle cuts are required, a diamond-bladed tub saw (see page 113) is the best bet.

Working with mortar. Though the most accurate way to apportion mortar ingredients is to weigh them, masons often mix by the shovelful. The key is to mix in small batches and to be consistent. A typical mix might be 1 shovelful of cement, 3 of sand, and ½ of lime.

You can mix mortar in a small power mixer or by hand in a square of plywood, in a wheelbarrow, or in a wooden mortar box. Mix the mortar in small batches so it won't dry out; plan to use up the batch within an hour.

Once the dry ingredients are well blended, start adding water. Be conservative—it's easy to add too much. The amount of water needed cannot be specified in advance; it depends entirely on the composition of the mortar and the absorption rate of the masonry units to be laid, factors which can vary according to the weather.

Ready for use, your mortar should have a smooth, uniform, granular consistency. It should spread well and stick to vertical surfaces, yet not smear the face of your work.

Site Preparation

Successful bricklaying depends on proper preparation of the base. The ground should be solid. If you have to lay bricks on fill, be sure it has settled for some time, preferably a year. The fill should always be wetted and tamped or rolled before you lay the bricks. A bit of dry cement powder will help hold fill in place.

You can also lay brick on an existing concrete slab that's clean and in good condition.

Make a careful study of aggressive plant root systems, especially if you're planning to lay bricks in mortar or if you're using a grid system such as those mentioned earlier. Exceptionally vigorous roots can disturb the best-laid patio.

You'll first lay out the base grade, taking into consideration the base required for the bricklaying technique you've chosen (see the following sections). If drainage is poor, you may also need to add a 4-inch gravel base (6 to 8 inches is best where the ground freezes). A layer of filter fabric over the gravel is optional: the fine mesh prevents the growth of weeds.

It's best to give a firm edge to this kind of paving, both for appearance and for permanent stability. Dimension lumber, railroad ties, invisible edgings, and poured concrete edgings (see pages 85–87) all work well for brick patios. If you're installing a curved brick edging, adjust joint spaces as required to take the bends.

How to Cut a Brick

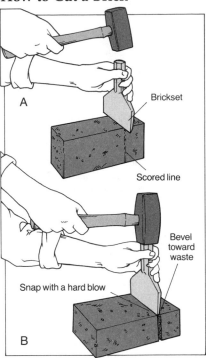

To trim a brick, use a brickset to score a line on all four sides (A); make the cut with one sharp blow (B).

Site Preparation

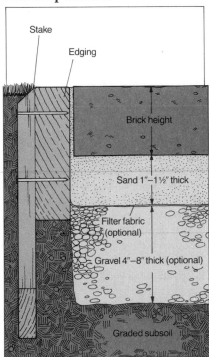

Typical brick-in-sand patio includes sand, optional gravel bed and filter fabric, plus wood edging.

Laying Bricks in Sand

A patio of brick-in-sand is one of the easiest paving projects for the beginner. With careful preparation and installation, this surface is as durable as bricks set in mortar and one that's as permanent as you want it to be. An added advantage: If you decide later to change the patio, you need destroy only one brick to get the rest out in perfect condition.

Typically, a 1- to 1½-inch-thick sand bed is prepared, and the bricks are laid with closed joints. You can set them with open ½-inch joints, but the surface will be less stable: the bricks can work themselves loose as the sand settles, requiring you to refill the joints from time to time. However, if you're using common brick that varies considerably in size, open joints may be the only answer.

How much to buy. The amount of materials you'll need to buy depends on the joints you're using. For 100 square feet of paving set with closed joints on a 1-inch bed of concrete sand, you'll need approximately 500 bricks and 9 cubic feet of sand. For the same size area set with ½-inch joints, buy about 450 bricks and 26 cubic feet of sand.

Grading the base. Lay out the base grade as discussed on pages 83–84. You don't need to be perfect—sand will take care of slight irregularities in the leveling process. Dump the gravel (if you're using it), rake it out evenly, and then tamp the base.

Edging. Build permanent wood or masonry edgings around the perimeter to hold both bricks and sand firmly in place. Or use temporary wood forms to hold a poured concrete edging until it hardens. For edge-building details, see pages 85–87.

If your design calls for one, add a permanent grid system. Plan to lay a

sample section before installing the grid permanently so you can check the fit and minimize brick cutting.

Screeding. An important operation, screeding is the leveling of sand to a uniform surface on which the bricks will rest. The screed rides on the edgings or temporary guides, leveling the sand as it's pulled along.

Make the screed from a 2 by 4; then nail on a plywood extension that's 2 inches or so shorter on both ends than the 2 by 4 and, for most edgings, exactly one brick thickness in width. For a wide patio where the screed won't reach between edgings, use a movable guide (a 2 by 6 set on edge) on which you can rest one end of the screed. Plan to work in 3-foot-

Laying Bricks in Sand

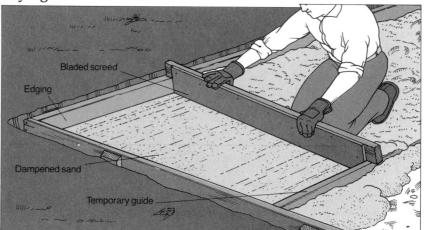

Once edgings are installed, lay down a 1- to 1½-inch-thick layer of damp sand. Level sand bed with a bladed screed, using a sawing motion as you go. If necessary, use temporary guides as shown.

Stretch a mason's line to help align courses; then, beginning from one corner, lay bricks tightly against one another, a course at a time, tapping each into place with a mallet or hammer.

wide sections, laying both sand and bricks in one section before moving on to the next.

Spread dampened sand in the first section and screed it smooth and level, using a sawing motion as you go. For a good, firm base, tamp the sand after screeding; add more sand, if needed, and screed again. An optional final pass with a steel trowel creates an extra-smooth surface. Don't walk on the base after the final screeding or troweling.

Setting bricks. Stretch a mason's line between edgings to aid in alignment and use a level often as you lay the bricks.

Working from one corner and following the pattern you've chosen, set the bricks into position, making sure they're tight against one another. (Don't slide them—you'll displace sand from the bed and trap it between the bricks.) Tap each brick into place with a rubber mallet or hammer.

Adding sand. When all the bricks are down to your satisfaction, you're ready to fill in the joints. Using fine sand, throw it out over the surface and let it dry for a few hours; then sweep it into the cracks. Wet the area with a light spray so that the sand in the joints will settle completely.

Laying Bricks with Dry Mortar

If you like the idea of open joints in brickwork but would prefer not having to rework the patio from time to time, use the dry mortar method. This paving provides a good, solid surface where subsoil is sound and severe frost is not a problem. The mortar also prevents weeds from coming up between the bricks and keeps water from washing away the foundation.

The bricks are set in the same way as bricks in sand with open joints, but you add Portland cement to the sand that is swept into the joints and then wet down the surface. (You also have the option of adding cement—in a 1:6 ratio—to the sand bed to keep the foundation from fraying at the edges and to stop the sand from disappearing down cracks in the ground.)

Note that although dry mortar isn't difficult to work with, some will usually stick to the bricks when you sweep it, leaving a mortar stain. This may not be a disadvantage if you like a rustic look.

How much to buy. For 100 square feet of paving with ½-inch joints on a 1-inch sand bed, you'll need approximately 450 bricks, 1 sack of cement, and 9 cubic feet of sand.

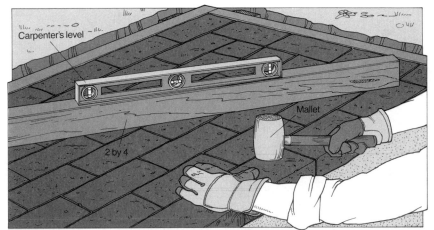

Check level often as you lay bricks, tapping any offenders down with a mallet. A straight 2 by 4 helps level bridge larger area. Remove temporary guides as you work; use a steel trowel to smooth sand.

Spread fine sand over surface of finished pavement, let it dry, and then sweep it into joints. Repeat until joints are filled. Finally, use a fine spray to wet finished paving down.

(Continued on next page)

Setting Bricks in Dry Mortar

Set bricks with ½-inch open joints. Spread dry mortar mix over surface, brushing it into joints.

½" plywood

Tamp mortar mix firmly into joints, using a piece of ½-inch-thick plywood. Sweep and dust surface before continuing.

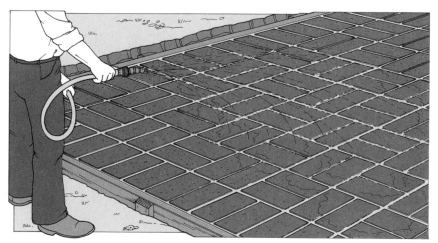

Using an extremely fine spray, wet down paving. During next 2 to 3 hours, wet paving periodically. Tool joints when mortar begins to harden.

Placing bricks and mortar. Following the directions for bricks in sand (see pages 94–95), lay and screed the sand bed; then set the bricks, leaving ½-inch joints (use ½-inch plywood and a mason's line for alignment). Check frequently with a level.

Prepare a dry mortar mix of 1 part cement and 4 parts sand. Kneeling on a piece of plywood to avoid disturbing the bricks, spread the mixture over the surface, brushing it into the joints. Tamp the mortar firmly with a piece of ½-inch plywood to improve the bond, adding more mix, if needed. Sweep and dust the bricks before continuing—any mix that remains may leave stains.

Wetting the surface. Using an extremely fine spray, wet the paving. Don't allow pools to form and don't splash the mortar out of the joints. During the next 2 to 3 hours, periodically wet the paving to keep it damp.

When the mortar begins to harden, you can smooth, or rake, the joints with a concave jointer or another rounded object to give the job a professional look.

Let the mortar set for about 2 hours; then scrub each brick with a wet burlap sack. Should further cleaning be necessary, wash the bricks with a solution of ½ cup each trisodium phosphate and laundry detergent in a gallon of water. Rinse well. If this doesn't work, try one of the methods discussed on page 138.

Laying Bricks in Wet Mortar

Brick paving set in mortar is a difficult job for the do-it-yourselfer. The method used by professionals—buttering each brick before setting it in place— requires much practice. But there's another procedure, explained here, that allows even the beginner to get handsome results.

How much to buy. For 100 square feet of paving with ½-inch mortar joints (not including the concrete base), you'll need approximately 450 bricks, 2 sacks of cement, and 12 cubic feet of sand.

Preparing the bed. You can either start with an existing concrete slab (it must be clean and in good condition) or pour a new foundation (for help, turn to pages 100–107). Add edgings, as described on pages 85–87; they should extend one brick thickness plus ½ inch (the thickness of the mortar bed) above the slab.

Wet the bricks several hours before you plan to use them to prevent them from sucking the water out of the mortar mixture. Then, using a mixture of 1 part cement and 4 parts sand, lay and screed a ½-inch-thick mortar bed between the edgings (add temporary guides where necessary). The screed should ride on the edgings and extend one brick thickness below them, as shown at top left. Mix only as much mortar as you can use in an hour or so, and screed only about 3 feet at a time.

Setting the bricks. Place the bricks in your chosen pattern, leaving ½-inch joints between them (use a piece of ½-inch plywood for a spacer and a mason's line for alignment). Gently tap each brick with a rubber mallet and check frequently with a level. Wait 24 hours before finishing the joints.

Grouting the joints. Use a pointed trowel to pack mortar (1 part cement to 4 parts sand, plus an optional ½ part hydrated lime to improve workability) into the joints, working carefully to keep mortar off the bricks. Let the joints harden for about 30 minutes. Finish them as for bricks in dry mortar (see facing page).

Keep the mortar damp for about 24 hours by covering bricks with a plastic sheet; stay off the bricks for 3 days.

Setting Bricks in Wet Mortar

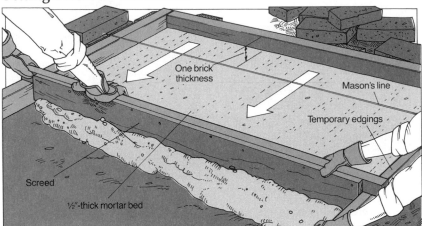

Screed a ½-inch-thick mortar bed between edgings set against slab. Edgings are one brick thickness plus ½ inch above slab; screed depth is exactly one brick.

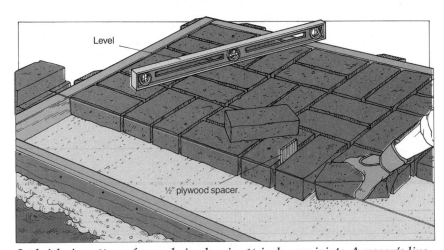

Set bricks in pattern of your choice, leaving ½-inch open joints. A mason's line helps align brick courses; wood spacers ensure even joints.

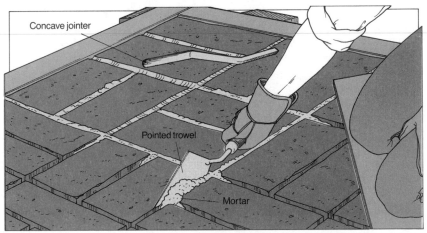

Pack mortar into joints, working carefully to minimize spilling. Wait about 30 minutes; then tool joints with a jointer or other rounded object.

ADDING A PATIO ROOF

Although there are many different designs for patio overheads, the basic components are the same—posts, beams, rafters (or joists), and some type of roofing.

The typical components of an attached patio roof are shown in the drawing on the facing page. Here is the basic building sequence; for help with design and building, consult a landscape professional.

Locating Footings

If your overhead spans an existing patio, you can set the posts on footings and piers located outside the edge of the patio, using ready-made piers on wet footings. Or you may have to break through the existing paving, dig holes, and pour new concrete footings and, if necessary, piers.

If you're installing a new concrete patio, pour footings and paving at the same time, embedding post anchors in the wet concrete.

Installing a Ledger

To attach the overhead to your house, you must install a ledger. Usually made of a 2 by 4 or a 2 by 6, the ledger is typically lag-screwed to the house framing (either to wall studs or, in a two-story house, to floor framing) or to the roof. Rafters can either sit on top of the ledger or butt against it.

If the house wall is masonry, you'll need to drill holes and install expanding anchors; then you bolt the ledger in place.

Setting Posts

Overheads are usually supported by 4 by 4 posts, though we show several more decorative options as well. Use either decay- and insect-resistant heartwood of redwood, cedar, or cypress, or less-expensive pressure-treated wood.

It's essential to measure post height accurately. For an attached overhead, your guide is the top of the ledger. Set a post in place temporarily; plumb and brace it. Run a mason's line from the top of the ledger to the post, level it, and mark the post. From this mark, subtract the slope of the roof (if any) plus the thickness of the beam, and make a new mark. Repeat with all other posts. Then take them down and cut them.

Set each post in place, check for plumb on two adjacent sides, and fasten the posts to the anchors. Making sure the posts are still plumb, nail on temporary braces.

Attaching Beams & Rafters

To secure beams, use post caps, beam clips, or framing clips. Before nailing, check that the beams are level and the posts vertical. If necessary, shim the posts with wood shingles wedged between the beam and post cap. Fasten the beams securely.

To attach rafters to the tops of the beams, either toenail them or, for a sturdier connection, use metal framing anchors. Rafters can also be notched to fit over beams. If you're using a ledger, toenail rafters to the top of the ledger, secure them with framing clips, or opt for joist hangers.

For patio roofs less than 12 feet high, normally only outside posts on unattached sides need cross bracing. Check your local building code for any exceptions in your area.

Adding a Roof

If an open effect is desired, the rafters can act as a roof. For more protection, attach wood lath 1 by 2s or 2 by 2s, spaced to give just the right amount of shade or arranged in a lattice pattern. Woven reed, canvas, and such solid roofing materials as shingles, tiles, and acrylic sheets can also be used.

Finishing Your Project

Sooner or later, wood's natural enemies—insects, weather, and decay-causing organisms—will attack any structure. Treating your patio roof with a preservative and/or finish can add years to the structure's life and keep it looking good.

Wood preservatives serve mainly as protection against decay; many have no effect on appearance. Finishes, usually paints or stains, protect against weathering. These do affect appearance—changing color, hiding wood grain, and sometimes even masking wood texture.

Patio Roof Anatomy

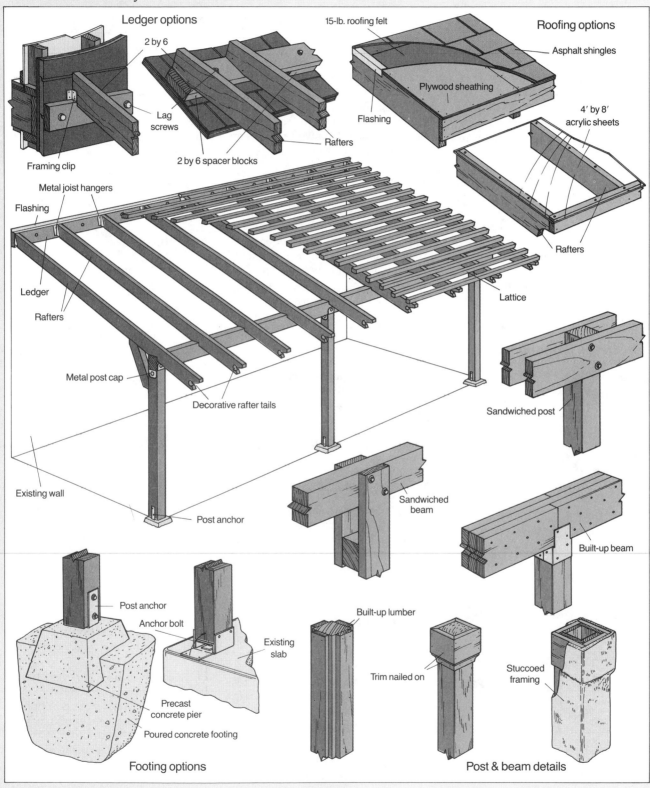

Ledger options

2 by 6

Lag screws

Framing clip

2 by 6 spacer blocks

Rafters

15-lb. roofing felt

Roofing options

Asphalt shingles

Plywood sheathing

Flashing

4' by 8' acrylic sheets

Rafters

Metal joist hangers

Flashing

Ledger

Rafters

Metal post cap

Decorative rafter tails

Lattice

Sandwiched post

Sandwiched beam

Built-up beam

Existing wall

Post anchor

Post anchor

Anchor bolt

Existing slab

Built-up lumber

Trim nailed on

Stuccoed framing

Precast concrete pier

Poured concrete footing

Footing options

Post & beam details

CONCRETE

Concrete is practical, serviceable, and surprisingly versatile. With concrete, you can create anything from small stepping-stones to sizable patio floors. You can texture it, color it, embed it with attractive stones, or make it resemble stone. Concrete also blends well with other "accent" materials, such as brick, tile, and stone.

A few words of caution: If you're paving a large area, divide the work into stages or sections that you and your helpers can handle. Plan ahead —getting ready for the pour will probably take more time than actually pouring and finishing the concrete. Remember that once concrete is in place, you're stuck with it; repair and replacement are costly and much more difficult than doing the job carefully and correctly in the first place.

Concrete Components

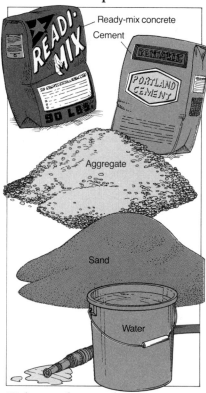

Either purchase ready-mix concrete (top left) or make your own from cement, aggregate, sand, and water.

Concrete Mixes & Formulas

Concrete is a mixture of Portland cement, sand, aggregate, and water. Cement is the "glue" that binds everything together and gives the finished product its hardness. The sand and aggregate (usually gravel) act as fillers and control shrinkage.

Buying concrete. Depending on how much time and money you're willing to invest, you can make up your own concrete mix from scratch, buy dry or wet ready-mix, or order transit mix from a concrete company.

Your choice should be based on the speed of the pour, which, in turn, is based partly on the size of the job and partly on the weather. If possible, the pour should be done all at once. If it's to be done in stages, plan to complete separate sections in single pours. Never interrupt a pour once it has begun, and remember that hot, dry weather will substantially shorten your available working time.

■ *Bulk dry materials.* If your project is fairly large, ordering materials in bulk and mixing them yourself is the most economical way to go.

■ *Dry ready-mix.* Buying bagged, dry ready-mix concrete is expensive, but it's also convenient, especially for small jobs. The standard 90-pound bag makes ⅔ cubic foot of concrete, about enough to cover a 16-inch-square area 4 inches deep.

■ *Wet ready-mix.* Some dealers supply trailers containing about 1 cubic yard of wet ready-mix concrete (about enough for an 8- by 10-foot patio). These trailers have either a revolving drum that mixes the concrete or a simple metal box into which the plastic concrete is placed. Both are designed to be hauled by your car.

■ *Transit-mix.* For a large patio, the best choice is a commercial transit-mix truck, which can deliver enough concrete to allow you to finish your project in a single pour. To locate concrete plants, look in the Yellow Pages under "Concrete—Ready Mixed."

Choosing a formula. For most residential wall and paving projects, the basic formula will give good results. In areas with severe freeze-thaw cycles, you'll need to add an air-entraining agent to prevent cracking.

■ *Basic concrete formula.* Use this formula for regular concrete (the proportions are by volume):

1 part cement
2½ parts sand
2¾ parts aggregate
½ part water

The sand should be clean river sand (not beach sand). The aggregate should range from quite small to about ¾ inch in size. The water should be drinkable—neither excessively alkaline nor excessively acidic, and containing no organic matter.

If you use a shovel to measure the dry ingredients, allow about 3 quarts of water for each 6 to 7 shovelfuls of cement.

■ *Air-entrained concrete.* Adding an air-entraining agent to the basic concrete formula creates billions of tiny air bubbles in the finished concrete, which help it to expand and contract without cracking. The agent also makes concrete more workable and easier to place. Because you add less water, the finished concrete is often stronger.

Ask your supplier how much agent to add to your concrete formula.

How much to buy. For every 10 cubic feet of finished concrete, you'll need the following amounts of bulk dry ingredients: 2.4 sacks of cement, 5.2 cubic feet of sand, and 7.2 cubic feet of gravel. If you're using ready-mix, buy .37 cubic yards for every 10 cubic feet.

If you order bulk materials sold by the cubic yard, remember that each cubic yard contains 27 cubic feet.

Tools for Concrete Paving

Shown at right are tools you're likely to have already—a wheelbarrow, a square-sided shovel, and a tape measure. Specialized mason's tools include a rectangular steel fanning trowel to finish the concrete surface, an edger to form smooth edges, a jointer to cut control joints, a wood float, and either a bull float (for large slabs) or a darby (for smaller jobs) to float the surface.

Preparing for the Pour

Like any paving, concrete requires a stable, well-drained base. But because the finished slab is monolithic, it's especially important to ensure that the ground beneath it doesn't shift and cause the concrete to crack.

Lay out and grade the site (see pages 83–84). If the exposed soil is soft, wet it and then tamp it firmly. Plan on at least a 2-inch gravel base in areas where frost and drainage are not problems, and a 4- to 8-inch base where they are. Don't add the gravel until after you've built and placed your forms.

Building & Placing Forms

The standard slab for pathways and patios is nominally 4 inches thick. But because 2 by 4s are generally used for forms, actual thickness will be 3½ inches if you use surfaced lumber. For a thicker slab (or a more rustic appearance), make the forms of rough, undressed lumber, which has slightly larger dimensions.

If you plan to leave the form lumber in place as permanent edgings

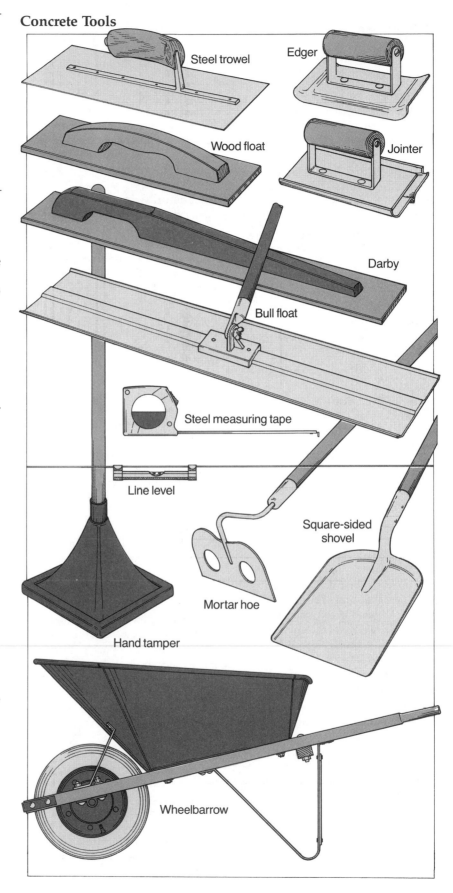

Concrete Tools

Steel trowel

Edger

Wood float

Jointer

Darby

Bull float

Steel measuring tape

Line level

Square-sided shovel

Mortar hoe

Hand tamper

Wheelbarrow

and dividers, use wood that's resistant to rot, such as the heartwood of redwood, cedar, or cypress, or pressure-treated lumber.

Straight forms. The easiest to build, straight forms can be assembled from standard lumber, either cut to length or spliced.

Screw or nail the forms to sturdy stakes driven into the ground at least every 4 feet. Drive the stakes plumb and deep enough so they won't rise above the top of the form and obstruct the screed. Wet concrete will exert considerable pressure on the forms, so be sure to fasten the corners securely and stake them well.

Drive 16d galvanized nails partway into the form about every 18 inches on the inside if you're leaving the form in place; this will lock the boards to the slab (see drawing at top of facing page). If you plan to strip the form, use double-headed nails to make disassembly easier.

Curved forms. Curved wood forms can be built by either bending or laminating.

Bending works best for gentle curves. For a temporary form, use tempered hardboard or plywood (with the outer grain running up and down) and bend it around stakes set on the inside edge of the curve. (Determine the radius with a pivoting board or straightedge, as described on page 84.) Where curved and straight sections meet, add extra stakes on both sides of the junction.

For an outside curve, first bend the wood around inside stakes and nail the ends to stakes set on the outside. Add more stakes on the outside, nailing the wood to them; then pull up the temporary stakes.

For very tight curves, cut sheet metal, plastic, or another flexible material to size and fasten it to the stakes. You may need extra stakes to ensure adequate support.

Use the laminating method if the curved form is to remain in place. Following the preceding directions, layer redwood benderboard around the stakes until the thickness is equal to your other form boards.

Expansion strips. If your patio or walk extends more than 20 or 25 feet in any direction and doesn't have permanent wood dividers, or you're pouring concrete up to an existing structure, you'll need to add expansion strips. These strips (available from building supply dealers) allow movement between adjoining sections of the slab or between two slabs, preventing cracking due to expansion and contraction.

First, make a movable stop board (see drawing on facing page, bottom right). Then, before pouring the slab, set the stop board in position with stakes and pour the concrete up to it. When the concrete has stiffened slightly, remove the board, set in a precut length of expansion-strip material, and continue pouring.

Reinforcement. Reinforcing concrete more than 8 feet square with steel mesh helps prevent cracking and will hold the pieces together if cracking does occur. Six-inch-square welded mesh is most commonly used.

Install the mesh after the forms are ready. Cut it to size with bolt cutters or heavy pliers, keeping it several inches away from the sides of the forms. Support the mesh on small stones, bits of brick, or broken concrete so that it will be held midway in the slab.

Preparing the forms. Before pouring the concrete, check your forms for level (or grade) and to be sure they're secure. Temporary forms should be oiled to aid in stripping; use motor oil or a commercial release agent. Cover tops of permanent forms with waterproof masking tape to prevent them from getting stained by the concrete.

Mixing Concrete

If you're mixing your own concrete, you can do it either by hand or with a power mixer. For small projects, hand-mixing is undoubtably the simplest method. But large forms that must be filled in a single pour may warrant a power mixer.

If you're using air-entrained concrete, you'll have to choose a power mixer; hand-mixing is simply not vigorous enough to create the air bubbles in the concrete mix.

Begin by mixing a small test batch so you can check and adjust proportions. Whatever method you use, add water in small amounts; too much can ruin the mix.

Hand-mixing. A high-sided contractor's wheelbarrow is adequate for mixing 2 cubic feet at a time. For larger batches, use a simple wooden platform or a mortar box (one measuring 53 by 25 by 11 inches will readily take up to 6 cubic feet of concrete). Add a sack of cement at a time.

Ingredients for small quantities of concrete are usually measured with a shovel—it's an accurate enough method if your scoopfuls are consistent. For greater accuracy, use a 1-cubic-foot wood box (make it bottomless for easy dumping—lifting the box empties the contents). Or empty a sack of cement into a bucket, level it, and then mark the bucket; this equals 1 cubic foot. If you also mark the bucket for ½ cubic foot, you'll find it easier to fill.

Mark a bucket off in quarts and gallons to keep track of the water. Set up so you can bail water from a drum or garbage can; it's more convenient than turning a hose on and off.

Mixing instructions. Following the proportions on page 100, place 2½ shovelfuls of sand on the mixing surface; add 1 shovelful of cement, mixing thoroughly. Then add about 3

Concrete Patio Overview

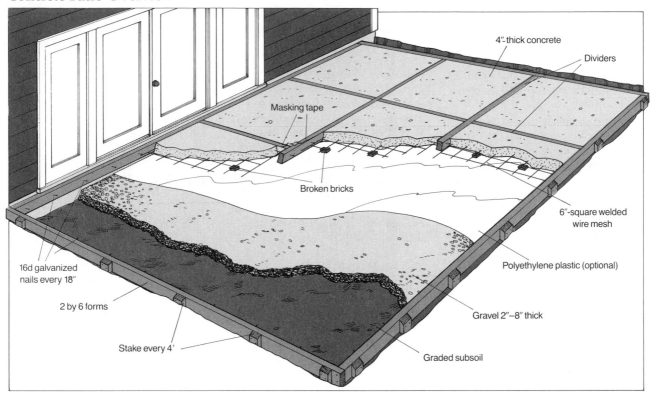

4"-thick concrete

Dividers

Masking tape

Broken bricks

6"-square welded
wire mesh

Polyethylene plastic (optional)

16d galvanized
nails every 18"

2 by 6 forms

Gravel 2"–8" thick

Stake every 4'

Graded subsoil

*Typical patio slab has 2 by 6 or 2 by 4 forms, either permanent or temporary. Gravel
bed promotes drainage; interior dividers create control joints and allow you to divide the pour into manageable increments. Welded wire mesh reinforces slab.*

Alternative Forms

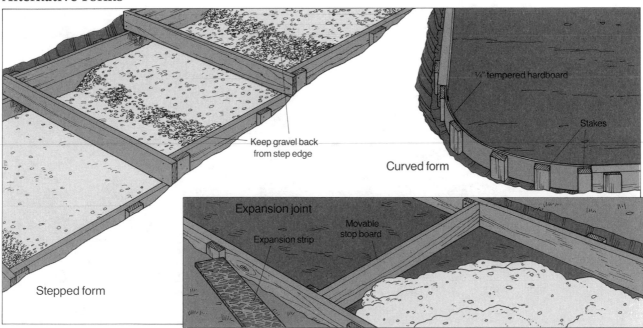

¼" tempered hardboard

Stakes

Curved form

Keep gravel back
from step edge

Expansion joint

Movable
stop board

Expansion strip

Stepped form

*Special patio shapes and dimensions call for special forms. Stepped form shown al-
lows you to negotiate a moderate slope; flexible hardboard strip shapes a sharp
curve. Expansion joints relieve stress on a wide, unbroken stretch of concrete.*

shovelfuls of gravel and mix again. Mound up the mixture and hollow out the center.

Pour in ½ quart of water; work around the hollow, pulling the dry ingredients into the water and always enlarging the size of the basin. Continue mixing until the color is uniform and all the ingredients are thoroughly moistened.

Machine-mixing. You can rent, borrow, or buy cement mixers in various sizes, but those under 3 cubic feet in capacity are uneconomical. (The mixer can be either electric- or gas-powered.) Set the mixer close to your sand and gravel piles so you can shovel-feed directly. Be sure the machine is level and chock it in place to prevent "walking."

■ *Mixing instructions.* To mix a small test batch, start the mixer (warm it up first if it's a gas one) and add a

little water. Then add, in order, a little gravel and sand, more water, more gravel and sand, and finally the cement. (Measure your ingredients by shovelfuls as you add them, but be sure not to put the shovel inside the mixer.)

Check the mix by pouring a little out—never look inside a mixer that's running. Mix just until all the ingredients are worked in and all the particles are wet.

The trial batch. Work a sample of your test batch with a trowel. The concrete should slide—not run—freely off the trowel, and you should be able to smooth the surface fairly easily, submerging the larger aggregates. Be sure that aggregates at the edges of the sample are completely and evenly coated with cement.

If your mix is stiff and crumbly, add a little water. If it's wet and soupy,

add a mixture of cement and sand, taking care that they're correctly proportioned. When you make adjustments, be sure to record them accurately; don't rely on "feel."

Pouring a Pavement

Whether you're making a single stepping-stone or pouring an entire patio, the basic steps are the same: you'll need to pour and spread the concrete, finish the surface, and then let it cure.

Before you begin, be sure you have enough hands for the job. Except for small projects, at least two people will be needed for most concrete work. Check that you have enough shovels and hoes to spread and tamp the concrete.

Don't neglect clothing, either. Rubber boots are important if you'll need

Pouring a Concrete Slab

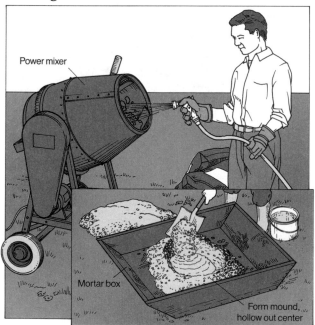

Choose a method of mixing based on your needs. Large jobs may require a power mixer; for smaller jobs, a mortar box (inset) or wheelbarrow is adequate.

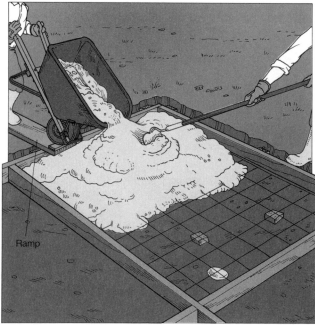

Start pouring concrete at one end of form while a helper spreads it with a hoe. Work concrete up against form and tamp it into corners.

to walk on the concrete to screed it, and gloves are essential to protect your hands from the caustic concrete.

One way forms can be filled is from a wheelbarrow—you can either shovel in the concrete or dump it in (you may need a ramp, as shown on facing page, at right). A splashboard will save concrete by letting you put it where you want it. If you're using a power mixer, you can pour the concrete directly from the drum (place the mixer next to the form).

If you're doing your own mixing, it's helpful to have one person mixing while others wheel and place the concrete. If you call for a transit-mix truck, you'll certainly need extra hands, especially if you have to move the concrete from one place to another.

Pouring, spreading, and tamping. Start pouring the concrete at one end of the form while a helper uses a shovel or hoe to spread it. Work the concrete up against the form and tamp it into all corners—don't simply rely on gravity.

Be sure not to overwork the concrete or spread it too far; overworking will force the heavy aggregate to the bottom of the slab and bring up the "fines"—inert silt that can cause defects in the finished concrete. Instead, space out your pours along the form, working each batch just enough to completely fill the form.

Striking off the concrete. To level the concrete, you'll need a screed, simply a long, straight board. On long pours, screed batch-by-batch rather than after all the concrete is placed.

Move the board slowly along the form, using a zigzag, sawing motion. Even on narrow forms, two people will speed the work and make it more accurate. A third person can shovel extra concrete into any hollows, as shown below, at left.

Floating. Initial floating, done immediately after strikeoff, smooths down high spots and fills small hollows left after screeding.

If you're using a bull float, as shown in the drawing below, push it away from you with its leading edge raised slightly and pull it back nearly flat. Overlap your passes.

Use a darby (shown in the inset below) on smaller projects. Move it in overlapping arcs; then repeat with overlapping straight, side-to-side strokes. Keep the tool flat, but don't let it dig in. On very small projects, a wood float can be used in a similar manner.

Edging and jointing. The first steps in finishing the floated surface to its

With a helper, move a screed across form to level concrete, using a rapid zigzag, sawing motion. A third person can shovel concrete into hollows.

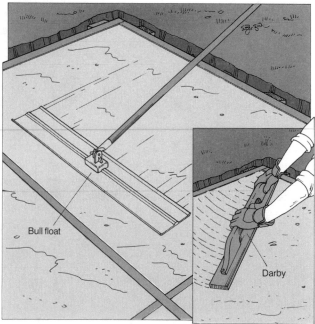

Initial floating smooths down high spots and fills small hollows left after screeding. Use a bull float for large areas, a darby (inset) for smaller ones.

final desired texture are edging and jointing.

Edging compacts and smooths the edges along the forms, creating a smoothly curved edge that will resist chipping.

Begin by running a trowel between the concrete and the form. Then follow up with the edger, keeping the forward edge of the tool tilted slightly upward. Edge again lightly after the final finish has been applied (except in the case of an exposed aggregate finish).

Jointing provides a guide for and induces cracking along a desired course when the concrete expands and contracts during temperature changes. (Permanent dividers serve the same purpose.) Control joints should be made in long walks at intervals no greater than 1½ times the width of the walk; in patio slabs, place control joints every 10 feet.

Use the edger or a special jointer with a straight board, as shown below, at right, to make control joints. Apply the same pressure and motion as with the edging tool.

Final floating and troweling. Unless you want a nonskid surface (see below), give the slab a final floating with a wood float after the water sheen has disappeared from the concrete but before the surface has become really stiff. Kneel on boards to reach the center of a large slab.

For a smoother surface, follow with a steel trowel. Make your initial passes with the trowel flat on the surface; use some pressure but don't let the blade dig in.

Creating a nonskid surface. For a nonskid surface, substitute brooming (shown on facing page, at right) for final floating and troweling. The texture

you produce will depend on the stiffness of the bristles and whether you use the broom wet or dry. The pattern can be straight or wavy, depending on how you move the broom.

Drag the broom over the concrete after edging and jointing, always pulling it toward you. Avoid overlapping passes; this knocks down the grain texture and produces "crumbs." Finish up by redoing the edges.

Curing. Hydration—a process whereby cement and water combine chemically—is the key to hardness in finished concrete. Care must be taken to ensure that this process proceeds slowly and completely: if water is allowed to evaporate too quickly from concrete, hydration will be incomplete, and the finished concrete will be weak.

You cure concrete by keeping it wet. To do this, cover the slab with

. . . Pouring a Concrete Slab

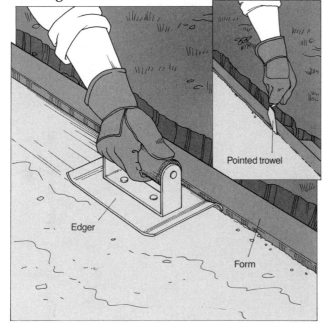

First, run edge of a trowel between concrete and form (inset). Follow up with an edger, running tool back and forth to create a smooth, curved edge.

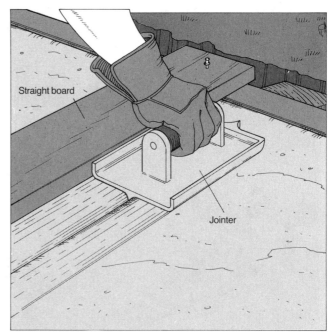

To make control joints, use an edger or a special jointer with a guide board, as shown. You'll need such joints every 10 feet in a patio slab.

straw, burlap, or another material that you can wet down as needed. Or you can cover the surface with plastic sheeting or a commercial curing compound; water evaporating from the concrete will be trapped, eliminating the need for wetting. If no covering material is available, you'll need to keep the surface damp by frequent hand-sprinkling.

Although the curing process may be complete in just a few days, it's a good idea to let the concrete cure for a week, just to be on the safe side.

Special Finishes

The appearance of a concrete surface can be altered to suit a variety of tastes (for some examples, see page 16). Here are some of the most widely used methods.

Exposed aggregates. The attractive exposed-aggregate finish is probably the most popular for residential concrete work. One way to produce it is to expose the regular sharp aggregate already present in the concrete (you'll get better results if you've used a uniform, coarse aggregate). A second method is to "seed" either a special aggregate or some smooth pebbles into the surface.

Take extra care in curing exposed-aggregate surfaces; the bond must be strong. Any cement haze left on the stones can be removed later with a 10 percent muriatic acid solution (see page 138).

■ *Exposing regular aggregate.* To expose the aggregate already in the concrete, pour and finish the slab through the floating stage. Don't over-float, or you may force the aggregate too deep. When the concrete has hardened to the point where it will just

support your weight on knee boards without denting, you can begin exposing the aggregate.

Gently brush or broom (nylon bristles are best) the concrete while wetting down the surface with a fine spray. Stop when the tops of the stones show. (If you dislodge stones, wait a little longer before brushing—the concrete isn't ready yet.)

■ *Seeding aggregate.* With the seeded-aggregate method, you can use the varicolored smooth pebbles that make this finish so popular.

Pour the slab in the usual manner, but strike it off about ½ inch lower than the form boards.

Distribute the aggregate evenly in a single layer over the slab (see drawing on page 108). Using a piece of wood, a float, or a darby, press the aggregate down until it lies just below the surface of the concrete. Refloat the

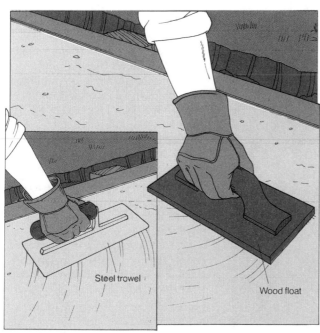

Before surface becomes really stiff, give it a final floating with a wood float. For a smoother surface, follow with a steel trowel (inset).

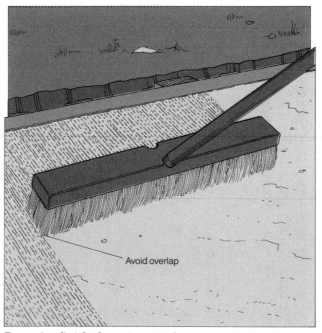

Brooming finished concrete produces a nonskid surface. Instead of using a float or trowel, drag a broom over concrete, always pulling it toward you.

concrete and then brush the slab as described for the exposed-aggregate method.

Salt finish. Coarse rock salt can be used to achieve a distinctive pocked surface on concrete. This finish is not recommended for areas with severe freezing weather. Water trapped in the pockets will expand upon freezing and may crack or chip the surface.

To produce this surface, scatter coarse chunks of rock salt over the surface of the slab after it has been floated; then press the salt chunks in with a float or trowel and wait for the water sheen to disappear. Depending on the smoothness you desire, finish the surface by troweling or wood floating. After curing the slab, simply wash out the salt with a strong spray of water.

Travertine finish. For a marbled effect, try the travertine finish, but not if you live where the ground freezes.

After striking and floating the concrete, roughen the surface slightly with a broom—or just leave it very roughly floated—to prepare it for the next step. Using a large brush, dash a 1:2 cement-sand mix unevenly over the surface. Coloring the mixture (see facing page) to contrast with the concrete heightens the effect.

When the slab can support you on knee boards, float or trowel the surface, knocking down the high spots. The result is a texture smooth in the high spots and rougher in the low spots. Cure the slab in the usual way.

Stamping or tooling. Concrete stamping makes a slab resemble brick, adobe, or stone. The stamping technique is simple, at least for a contractor. First, a regular concrete slab is poured and floated smooth. (Often the slab is colored, usually by the dusting method described on the facing page.)

After floating, a special grid of patterned stamps is pressed into the slab. Workers stand on the grids to force them into the concrete. A final going-over with a trowel fixes any blemishes, and the project is cured in the usual manner. The stamped "joints" can be left as is or mortared to resemble regular mortar joints.

A more homespun way to break up a dull expanse of plain concrete is to tool the freshly floated concrete so that it resembles flagstone. Use a concave jointer; or bend an offset in a short length of ½- to ¾-inch copper pipe to make a good tool for this work. Sketch your pattern in advance and work from the plan. Erasures are awkward, so you need a sure hand.

When the water sheen has disappeared, do the final floating or troweling and redo the tooling. Trowel again if you want a very smooth finish. Touch up the surface with a soft brush and cure the slab.

Seeded-aggregate Finish

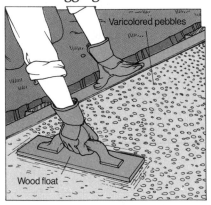

After screeding, spread aggregate over surface in a single layer; embed with a darby or piece of wood.

Float slab; then brush and hose surface gently once it's stiff enough. Be careful not to dislodge stones.

Salt Finish

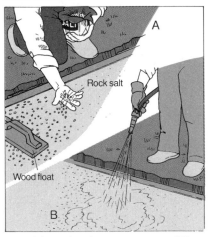

Sprinkle rock salt over concrete (A), embedding it with a float; hose out salt (B) after curing slab.

Travertine Finish

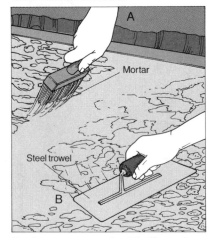

Dash mortar over freshly floated slab, using a large brush (A). Trowel or float (B) after slab has stiffened.

Coloring Concrete

One of the easiest masonry products to tint, concrete can be very colorful. To add color to concrete, you can mix color pigments into wet concrete before it's poured, dust color pigment on the surface during the finishing process, or apply stain or paint to the paving after it's completely dry.

Mix-in color. Mix the pigment with the cement and aggregate in a dry state first. Using white Portland cement will produce brighter coloration; save the gray cement for black and dark gray tones. The best way to proportion the pigment is by weight: the pigment should never exceed 10 percent of the weight of the cement. To assure uniform coloration, keep this weight proportion consistent from one batch to the next.

With this method, you can either pour an entire slab of colored concrete mixture or pour a conventional slab first, leaving the surface rough, and then cover it with a 1-inch slab of the colored mix.

Dust-on color. To apply color this way, first prepare the concrete surface through the wood-floating process; then spread two-thirds of the amount of color specified by the manufacturer and float the surface. Apply the remaining mixture, float again, and finish with a light troweling. Be sure to edge and regroove the joints after each application.

Brush-on color. Use this method to apply color—in the form of stain or paint—to the concrete surface after it has hardened. It makes no difference whether the surface is weeks or years old, but it must be very clean. To do a thorough job, clean the surface with a solution of trisodium phosphate and warm water, scrubbing with a wire brush (be sure to wear gloves). Then flush with clear water.

Avoid painting the concrete when it has been heated by the sun.

■ *Stains.* The most durable of the brush-on colors, stains are relatively easy to apply. Semi-transparent wood stains work particularly well on concrete.

Don't stain new concrete unless it has cured for at least 6 weeks. After cleaning, apply the stain with a roller or brush; add a second coat for a darker color.

■ *Paints.* Paints provide the widest choice in colors. Water-base latex paint is one of the best kinds to use, but others are also suitable.

After cleaning the surface, you may want to etch it with a 10 percent muriatic acid solution. Roll or brush on two or three coats of paint.

Stamping & Tooling

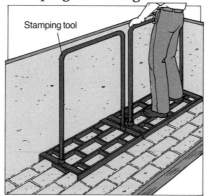

Stamping tool

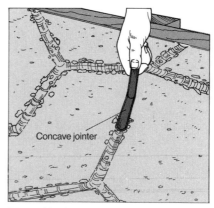

Concave jointer

Stamping is performed by body weight; you'll need two tools so you can step off one onto the other.

To tool by hand, work surface with a concave jointer or pipe. Float again; then smooth blemishes with a trowel.

Coloring Concrete

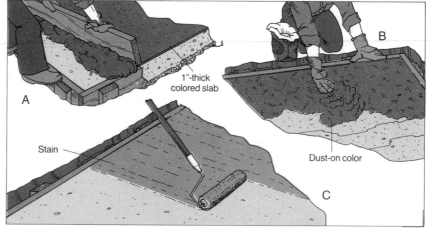

A

1"-thick colored slab

B

Stain

Dust-on color

C

To add color to a new slab, screed on a top coating of colored concrete (A), spread and float a dust-on mixture (B), or apply stain or paint with a roller or brush (C).

INSTALLING A PATIO DOOR

When designing your new patio environment, don't forget the importance of convenient access. Two types of doors—French and sliding—are the traditional choices for connecting indoor and outdoor living spaces.

To avoid the rigors of traditional door-hanging, you can buy a prehung set of doors, placed inside a frame with exterior trim in place. Or you can buy a factory-assembled unit, completely weatherstripped and finished on the exterior, with threshold and sill included. You need only cut into the wall and frame the new opening.

Here is the basic sequence you'll need to follow for installing a patio door. For help, consult a professional.

Locating the Opening

Before choosing the exact location for your doors, check the wall carefully. If it's a bearing wall or if it conceals any complex heating, plumbing, or electrical systems, you may want to call in a professional.

Before starting work, check the manufacturer's "rough opening" dimensions—the exact wall opening required for the door and jambs after the rough framing members are in place. Or simply add ½ inch all around the unit for shimming (adjusting level and plumb).

For a view of a typical door opening, see the drawing on the facing page.

Removing the Interior Wall

It's best to locate the doorway so you can use at least one of the existing wall studs as a king stud at the outside of the opening. If the wall is a bearing one, you must install a temporary support (shown at right) under the ceiling joists, parallel to the wall section being removed, before you cut the opening.

Mark the proposed opening on the wall; then remove the interior wall covering from floor to ceiling. Before cutting the studs within the opening to the height required for the header, double-check the rough opening dimensions, being sure to add the rough framing depth needed.

Using a combination square, mark the studs to be cut on their faces and on one side; sever them carefully with a reciprocating or crosscut saw. Pry the cut studs loose from the sole plate, leaving their top portions (called cripple studs) in place.

Installing the Framing

Measure and cut two trimmer studs and nail one to each king stud with 10d nails in a staggered pattern. Then measure and cut a 4-by header or build a "sandwich" from two lengths of 2-by lumber and a ½-inch plywood spacer (the exact width of your header stock depends on the size of the opening

Support for a Bearing Wall

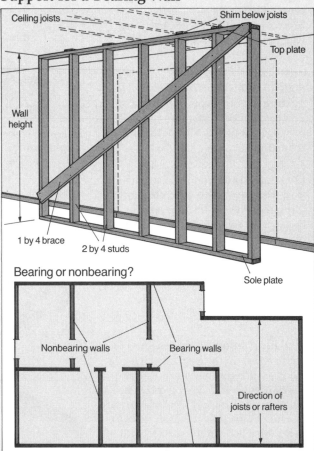

Shore up cuts into bearing walls with a temporary support (top). How can you tell a bearing wall? It holds up joists or rafters at their ends or at midspan.

and on local codes). Toenail the header to the king studs with 16d nails; then toenail the cripples to the header with 8d nails.

To adjust the opening's width, nail a pair of trimmers on one side to the header and sole plate.

Opening Up the Outside

On a clear day, drill a hole through the wall from the inside at each corner of the rough opening. Stick a long nail through each hole so you can find the corners outside. From the outside, mark the rough opening with a pencil and level. Then, using a reciprocating or circular saw, cut through the siding and sheathing. Finally, cut through the sole plate and pry it up.

Check your local building code for any flashing required around the opening. Typical flashing materials are galvanized steel and roofing felt. Work the flashing behind the siding; then fold it over the new framing, overlapping at all corners.

Installing the Unit

Installation of both French and sliding doors is similar. Fit the door and frame unit into the rough opening, shim it plumb and square, and firmly screw or nail it to the wall framing. Caulk the seams where the outside casing meets the siding; you may also wish to install an apron, as shown below at right.

Attach the interior trim, patch the inside and outside wall coverings, and, if necessary, paint.

An Installation Overview

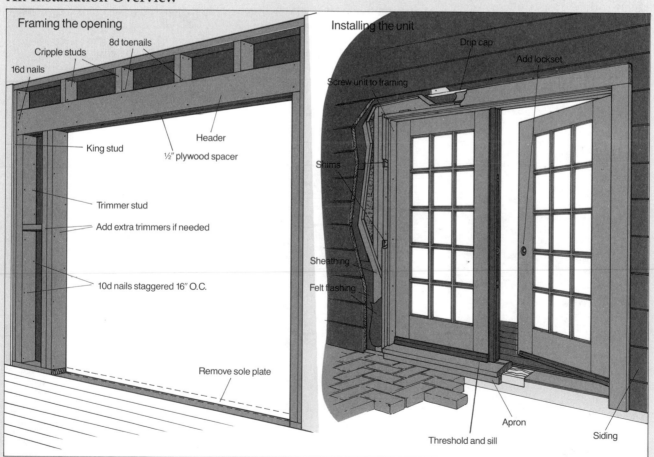

Door framing includes king studs, trimmer studs, cripple studs, and a built-up header (left). Slip prehung unit (right) into opening, plumb and square it, then fasten to new framing.

CONCRETE PAVERS

For the do-it-yourselfer, concrete pavers are an ideal patio material—durable, relatively inexpensive, and easy to lay. And as you can see from the photos on pages 20–22, they come in a variety of shapes and sizes.

Pavers are available at most building and garden supply centers. Costs vary according to size and texture. For example, a 12-inch square of 1½-inch-thick concrete seeded with pebbles can cost three times as much as a plain or colored paver of the same dimensions.

Interlocking pavers fit together like puzzle pieces. They're available in tan, brown, red, and natural gray, plus blended colors. Some even have holes in them for planting—ideal for grassy parking areas. Unlike pavers made simply of poured concrete, these are poured and then compressed, giving them greater strength.

Interlocking pavers are laid in sand, just like brick; alignment is nearly automatic. Regular (noninterlocking) concrete pavers are also used just like brick, but these can be set in either sand or dry mortar.

Preparing the Site

Beneath the pavers, you'll need a 1- to 1½-inch-deep base of concrete sand—and for colder climates or pavings doubling as driveways, a deeper subbase of crushed gravel and filter fabric (see drawing on page 93). If you must excavate for a path or patio, allow for the thickness of both the pavers and the base. Be sure to provide for adequate drainage and grade (for help, see pages 82–84).

You can let pavers "run wild" into the surrounding landscape, but containing them within edgings (see pages 85–87) will help prevent shifting. Since edgings are installed first, they also serve as good leveling guides for preparing the base and laying the pavers.

Wood and poured concrete are the most popular edging materials for use with concrete pavers. If you choose wood, professionals recommend using 2 by 6s instead of 2 by 4s.

Another alternative is plastic edgings, shown on page 87. Rigid strips are best for a rectangular patio, but they'll also follow curves if kerfed with a hacksaw. Flexible sections handle tight turns. Set plastic edgings below finished paving height.

You'll have less cutting to do if you design a square or rectangular patio area that allows you to use full pavers. Special edging pieces, available for some interlocking patterns, eliminate border cutting altogether.

Laying Pavers

Most pavers are heavy and rough. You'll want a sturdy wheelbarrow to move them and heavy work gloves to protect your hands.

Setting Pavers in Sand

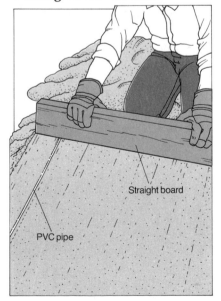

Push lengths of PVC pipe into sand bed; screed more sand to height of pipes' tops.

Remove pipes; then lay interlocking pavers one at a time, snugging them into position with a mallet.

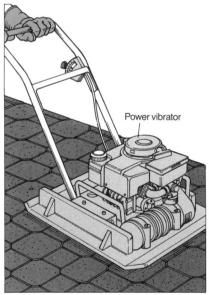

Check level as you go; once all pavers are down, use a power vibrator to settle them.

If you have to cut a few pavers, you can probably do the job with a brickset, cutting them in the same way as brick (see page 93). But for numerous or complex cuts, rent a tub saw fitted with a diamond blade. To save on rental fees, lay all the pavers first, positioning and marking the ones to be cut, and setting them aside. Then do all your cutting at once (be sure to wear safety goggles).

Laying pavers in sand. If your design calls for permanent edgings, prepare the sand bed and lay the pavers as for bricks in sand (see pages 94–95). If you've chosen wood or concrete edgings, use a bladed screed set at exactly one paver thickness in depth; for plastic or other recessed edgings, set screed depth about 1 inch less.

Another method of laying interlocking pavers in sand—with or without edgings—is to set out lengths of PVC pipe, 1 to 1½ inches in diameter, several feet apart over a sand bed.

Push the pipes into place; add more sand. Then use a straight board (see drawing on facing page, far left) to level the sand at the height of the pipes' tops.

Remove the pipes and smooth over the depressions. Lay the pavers, snugging them into position with a mallet and checking frequently with a level. Then make several passes with a power plate vibrator to settle them. Vibrating in a final layer of sand will help lock the pavers together.

Laying pavers in dry mortar. For a slightly more stable patio with a more formal look than you can get from a sand base only, consider the dry mortar method (suitable for all except interlocking pavers).

Essentially, you space the units a uniform distance apart (butt them against ⅜-inch plywood, as shown below, at center, to ensure even spacing), and then set and pack them as for pavers laid in sand. But instead of sweeping sand into the joints, you

add a sand-and-cement mortar mix, just as for bricks set in dry mortar (see pages 95–96). Expect some discoloration in the finished patio project.

Cutting with a Tub Saw

A rented tub saw cuts edging pavers; wear eye protection and keep hands well away from blade.

Using Dry Mortar

Sweep fine sand into paver joints; compress sand with additional passes of vibrator or roller.

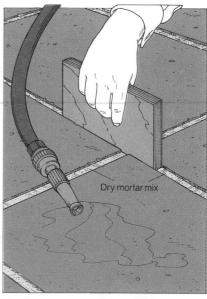

Set pavers with open joints on a sand bed; then sweep dry mortar mix into spaces.

⅜" plywood spacer

Dry mortar mix

Pack mortar into joints with a piece of wood, wet down mix, and tool with a jointer or similar tool.

Sand

In-ground Molds

Dig a series of closely spaced holes, keeping sides sharply cut and fairly vertical.

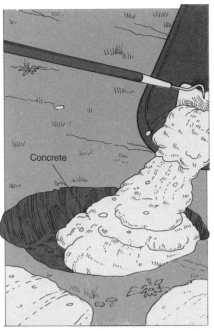

Concrete

Fill each hole with concrete, carefully screed off excess, and finish surface as desired.

A Potpourri of Paving Blocks

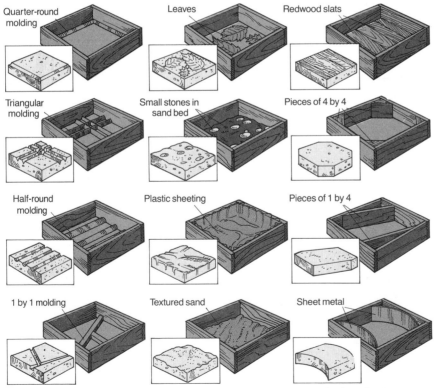

Quarter-round molding

Leaves

Redwood slats

Triangular molding

Small stones in sand bed

Pieces of 4 by 4

Half-round molding

Plastic sheeting

Pieces of 1 by 4

1 by 1 molding

Textured sand

Sheet metal

A simple 2 by 4 frame allows you to cast your own paving blocks; placing a bottom in the box can lead to all sorts of interesting designs, as shown above. If you're casting lots of pavers, a multiple-grid form will speed up the job.

Casting Your Own Pavers

For a distinctive look that's just right for your needs, consider making your own pavers. Two molding methods are described below. Before you begin, be sure you're familiar with the techniques for working with concrete (see pages 100–109).

In-ground molds. The easiest way to make stepping-stones and free-form concrete pads is to pour them in place in the ground, as shown at left.

Dig a hole 4 inches deep for each "stone," contouring it as you choose. For easy walking, space the steps no more than 18 inches apart. If you're working in a lawn, plan to keep the tops of the stones below ground level to allow for mowing.

Fill the holes with a 1:2:3 cement-sand-aggregate mixture. Tossing in a few stones as filler saves concrete. Finish the tops with a trowel or wood float; then cure.

To enhance the look, you may want to try the travertine finish. Integral colors and concrete stains offer a rainbow of other options.

Closed-frame molds. For more uniformly edged pavers, cast your blocks in a mold you make yourself (for some examples, see drawing at left).

A simple closed frame made of 2 by 4 lumber or any sturdy wood is the simplest to construct. For ease in unmolding, hinge two corners, adding a hook and eye to secure the corner. If you need lots of pavers, a multiple-grid form will speed up the job.

Oil the form with motor oil or a commercial release agent and place it on a smooth surface. Fill it with a stiff concrete mix, packing in the concrete. Screed with a straight board. You can float the surface if you like or use the block's smooth underside for the stepping surface.

Let the concrete set for a few hours before unmolding; then cure.

CERAMIC TILE

Laying tile is well within the capabilities of the home mason, but it cannot be done quickly. Because tiles are such precise building units, the slightest flaws in installation may be noticeable, so plan your work carefully.

Grade the site very carefully (see pages 82–84); a flat laying bed is crucial. Depending on the tile you choose, you can set the units in sand, in dry mortar, or in wet mortar. If you're using the last method, take care not to stain the tiles with mortar.

Laying Out Tile

Tiles suitable for exterior use are available in a variety of colors and sizes; for help in choosing one that will be compatible with your patio design, see the first chapter.

Carefully measure the area to be covered. Calculate the number of tiles you need to buy according to the size you've chosen. (Unless you're butting tiles in a sand bed, be sure to allow for joints.) It's a good idea to buy tiles in large lots; if you have to buy more later, the colors may not match. Mix the tiles from box to box as you work to ensure a consistent look.

If you must cut a lot of tiles to complete a pattern or fill in an oddly shaped space, it's easiest to mark the cutting lines and have them sawn at a masonry yard equipped with a diamond-bladed saw. For do-it-yourself cutting, a rented tub saw (see page 113) is the best choice; but if you have only a few cuts, a portable circular saw and masonry cutting blade (see drawing on page 116), or a snap cutter, which can be rented from a tile dealer, will also do the job. Use tile nippers for irregular shapes, first scoring the cutting lines with a small glass cutter.

If your paving calls for a curved edge, cut the tiles in a series of angles that correspond roughly with the curve. You can also lay a curved rim

of bricks on top of the tile to give the appearance of a curved edge.

Laying Tile in Sand

Heavy tiles—tiles that are at least ¾ inch thick—can be laid in sand. Level the soil to allow for a ½-inch sand bed plus the thickness of the tile. Build permanent edgings (see pages 85–87) to hold the tiles in place, setting the edgings so their tops will be flush with the finished surface.

Lay a bed of damp sand, leveling it with a bladed screed (shown below) that moves along the edgings. (One cubic foot of sand will cover about 20 square feet ½ inch deep.) Screed about 3 feet at a time, moving any temporary guides along. For a firm base, tamp the sand after screeding; add more sand and screed again.

For extra stability, you can add dry cement to the setting bed—1 part cement to each 8 parts sand. Before mixing, sift the cement through household screening.

Lay tiles with either open joints (½ inch for small tiles, ¾ inch for larger ones) or closed joints (tiles butted tightly together).

Starting at a corner, set the tiles in place, tapping with a rubber mallet to bed them in the sand. Check for level as you go.

Throw fine sand over the surface. After it dries, sweep it into the joints, filling all of them. Finally, wet the area with a fine spray.

Laying ¾-inch Tile in Sand

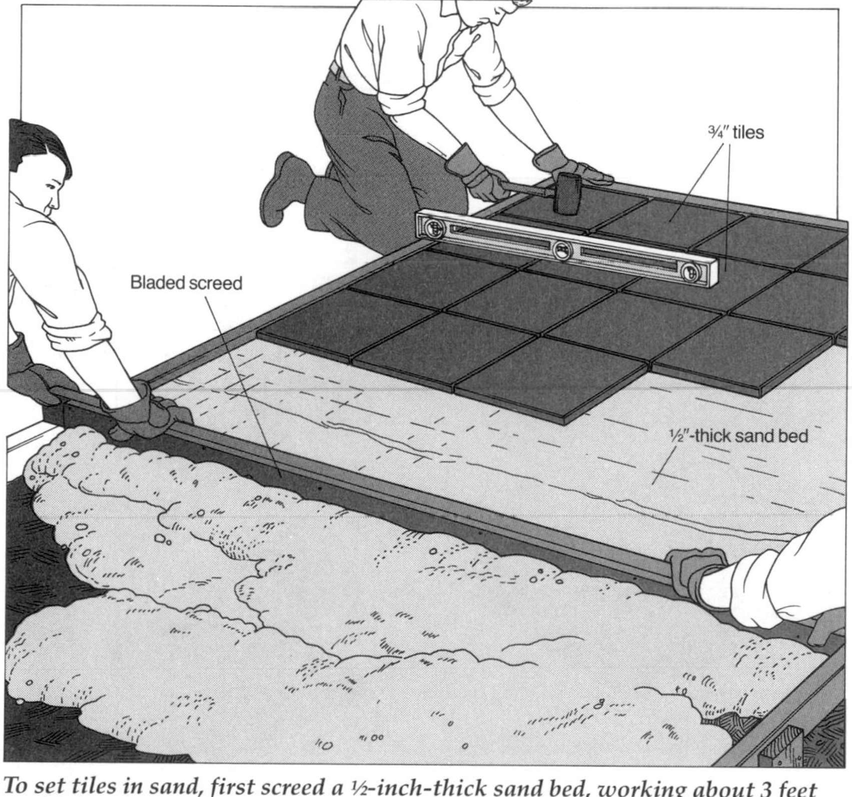

To set tiles in sand, first screed a ½-inch-thick sand bed, working about 3 feet at a time. Beginning in one corner, set tiles, tapping them with a rubber mallet and checking with a level. Sweep sand into joints. Wet with a fine spray.

Setting Tile in Wet Mortar

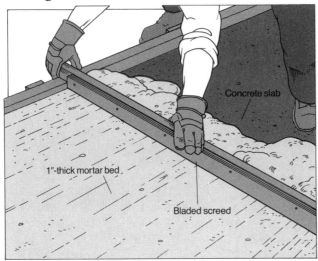

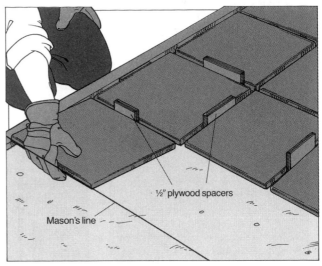

Position edging boards against a concrete slab; then float a 1-inch-thick mortar bed, leveling it with a bladed screed.

Beginning in one corner, set tiles in place, leaving ½-inch open joints. Check level as you work.

CERAMIC TILE

Laying Tile in Wet Mortar

Shown above is a particularly stable method of laying tile—in a 1-inch mortar bed over an existing concrete slab or a newly poured one (for basic concrete techniques, see pages 100–107). If you're using an old slab, wash it with a diluted muriatic acid solution. Clean and rinse well. Then brush a coat of cement and water paste over the surface.

Install permanent or temporary edgings; they should rise above the concrete base one tile thickness plus an inch for the mortar bed. Lay a stiff, 1:4 cement-sand mortar bed on the concrete, leveling it with a bladed screed.

Then lay the tiles, leaving ½-inch open joints (use pieces of plywood for spacers and a mason's line for alignment). Tap the centers with a rubber mallet and check frequently with a level. Let the mortar set for 24 hours.

Prepare a 1:3 cement-sand mixture for the joints; it should be just thin enough to pour. Using a bent can, fill the joints, cleaning away spills immediately with a damp sponge. When the grout begins to harden, tool the joints as shown, using a concave jointer or a similar tool. Keep the mortar damp for the first day by covering it with a plastic sheet and stay off the paved area for 3 days.

Cutting Tile

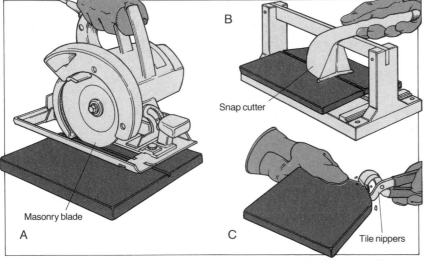

A tub saw with a diamond blade is the best way to cut tiles, but a circular saw and masonry blade (A) or a snap cutter (B) will work, too. Nibble curves with tile nippers (C).

Laying Tile in Dry Mortar

Level the soil 3 inches plus one tile thickness below the desired grade of the paved surface and build temporary wood guides around the area. Set the tops of the guides so they'll be

Let tiles set for 24 hours. Prepare a sand-cement grout mixture and pour into tile joints from a bent can.

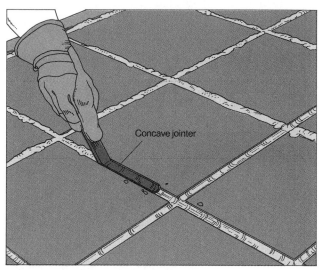

Once grout begins to set, work it with a concave jointer or a homemade tool, such as a broom handle or pipe.

flush with the surface of the tiles. Pack soil around the guides.

Lay a 3-inch-thick sand bed and level it between the guides with a bladed screed; set the blade for the thickness of one tile. Over every 100 square feet of surface, distribute 2 bags of cement. Rake the sand and cement together, being careful not to mix in the soil below; then tamp and rescreed the mix to a smooth surface.

Evenly sprinkle the bed with half a bag of cement for every 100 square feet. Lay the tiles as for tiles set in wet mortar (see facing page), except leave ⅜-inch open joints.

Wet the area with a fine spray. Don't let pools form and don't splash mortar out of the joints. Let the tiles set for 24 hours; then grout them as for tiles set in wet mortar.

Laying Tile over Wood Flooring

You can use tile to cover a wood stairway, deck, or porch with pleasing results, provided that your structure can support the added weight without sagging (patio tile on a 1-inch mortar

bed weighs about 20 pounds per square foot). Also, the surface must support foot traffic without flexing. If you have any doubt, install additional support before laying the tiles.

Nail a layer of waterproof building paper over the flooring. Then stretch a

reinforcing mesh of ¾-inch chicken wire and nail it down, leaving ¼ inch between the wire and the surface.

Apply a 1-inch mortar bed, using a 1:5 cement-sand mixture. Dust with a layer of cement. Lay the tiles; grout them as for tiles set in wet mortar.

Laying Tile over a Wood Surface

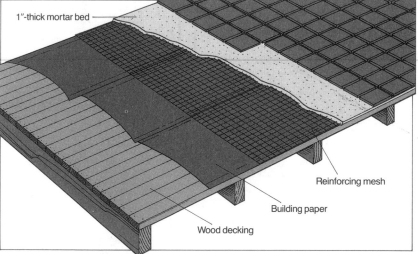

1"-thick mortar bed

Reinforcing mesh

Building paper

Wood decking

If framing and drainage are satisfactory, tile can be laid over a wood deck or rooftop. Building paper and wire mesh form the membrane; tiles are set in a 1-inch mortar bed and grouted.

LOW-VOLTAGE OUTDOOR LIGHTING

Installing a low-voltage lighting system outdoors is relatively simple: cable can lie on the ground (perhaps hidden by foliage) or in a narrow trench, and no electrical permit is required, provided the system extends from a plug-in transformer, the most common kind. Moreover, there's much less danger that people or pets will suffer a harmful shock from a low-voltage system than from a 120-volt one.

To install a 12-volt system, you'll need at least one transformer (large patios and garden areas may require several), two-wire outdoor cable, and a set of 12-volt fixtures. To activate the system, you connect the transformer, and perhaps a separate switching device or timer, to an existing power source. A typical low-voltage lighting system is illustrated on the facing page.

CAUTION: *Never* work on any "live" circuit, fixture, receptacle, or switch. Before beginning work, shut off the appropriate circuit at the service entrance panel or subpanel.

Planning the Installation

You can buy low-voltage systems in kit form; most come with transformers appropriate for the number of lamps in the kit, which means that you cannot add more lights. Or, you can buy the components separately.

To determine what size transformer you need, add the total number of watts used by all the lamps you plan to connect (for safety, use only 80 percent of a transformer's capacity to avoid overloading). Some transformers come with internal fuses or circuit breakers; others must have fuse boxes added to the circuit.

Although many transformers have built-in switches, some do not. Consider installing a separate switch or low-voltage dimmer indoors for convenience.

Timers are another basic option. Some types are clock controlled; others are triggered by a remote photoelectric light cell.

For installation help or advice, consult a professional electrician.

Wire Thickness

Most low-voltage outdoor fixtures use stranded wire cable. The size of the wire depends on the aggregate wattage of the fixtures to be served. Here are the appropriate sizes for some typical wattages:

Wiring a GFCI

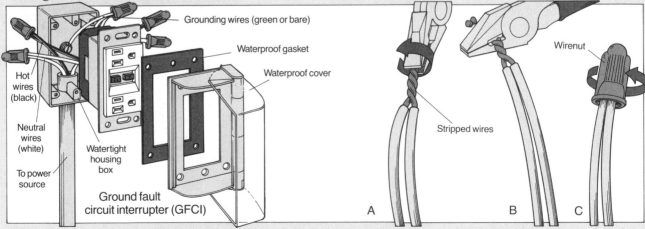

Ground fault circuit interrupter (at left) protects outdoor lighting circuit. GFCI is wired in same way as a standard receptacle. Strip 1 inch of insulation from wires to be joined and twist them clockwise 1½ turns (A), snip off ⅜ to ½ inch of wire (B), and screw wirenut on clockwise (C).

#14 wire—up to 144 watts
#12 wire—up to 192 watts
#10 wire—up to 288 watts

Avoid wires longer than 100 feet: the voltage drops too much for the lamps to operate at full potential. In a large garden, position standard-voltage outlets in remote locations and tie the transformers in at those spots.

Installing a Transformer

Most transformers for outdoor lights are encased in watertight boxes; still, to be safe, plan to install yours in a sheltered location at least a foot off the ground.

If you don't already have an outlet outside, install one equipped with a ground fault circuit interrupter (GFCI). This device works like a standard receptacle but cuts off power within 1/40 of a second if current begins leaking anywhere along the circuit.

The drawing on the facing page shows how to wire an outdoor GFCI. To make the connections, strip 1 inch of insulation from the wire ends, twist them clockwise 1½ turns, and snip off ⅜ to ½ inch. Screw a plastic wirenut clockwise onto the wires. Finally, twist a short "jumper" wire from the box's grounding screw together with the other two grounding wires and cap with a wirenut. If this is the end of the run, snip off any remaining outgoing wires from the GFCI and cover them with wirenuts.

To join one or more low-voltage cables to the transformer, wrap the bare wire ends of each cable clockwise around the screw terminals on the transformer—if the transformer accommodates more than one cable, the terminals will come in pairs—and tighten the terminals. It makes no difference which wire connects to which terminal in each pair.

Connecting Fixtures to Cable

With some fixtures, you simply pierce the cable with a screw-down connector attached to the back of the fixture. With others, you must screw an unattached clamp connector to the main cable and to the end of a short cable leading from the fixture. Neither method requires stripping the cable.

Some fixtures must be spliced into the main cable with wirenuts. Use watertight plastic housing boxes to insulate splices that can't be pushed back into the fixtures. The junction box in the illustration allows you to route wire in several directions from one protected location.

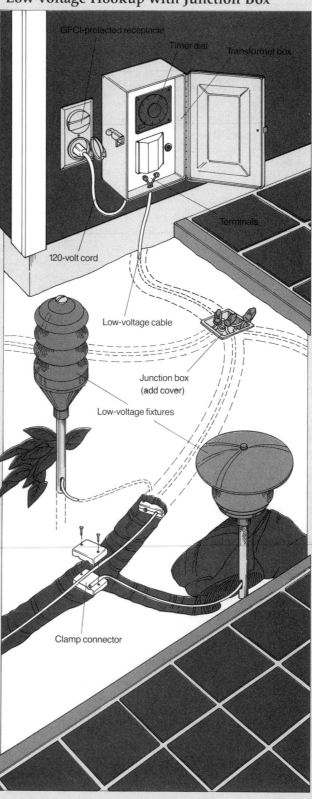

Low-voltage Hookup with Junction Box

GFCI-protected receptacle

Timer dial

Transformer box

Terminals

120-volt cord

Low-voltage cable

Junction box (add cover)

Low-voltage fixtures

Clamp connector

ADOBE

It's hard to match adobe for friendly, rustic charm. Today's adobe blocks contain an asphalt stabilizer that makes them waterproof and nearly as durable as brick. Because the blocks are large, construction proceeds quickly and your efforts yield immediate results.

Although adobe construction is found almost entirely in the Southwest, where manufacturing facilities are located, it can be used effectively anywhere.

Shopping for Adobe

If you live fairly close to a source of supply, adobe can cost less per square foot than brick. However, if you live outside the West, delivery charges may add considerably to the cost.

Most adobe is sold through dealers (check the Yellow Pages under "Building Materials"). Be sure to inquire about delivery arrangements.

Always buy at least a dozen extra adobe blocks—a few are likely to come with irregularities or will develop flaws after you put them down. Matching their color and texture later on may be difficult.

Setting Adobe Blocks

Laying adobe in sand allows for good drainage and extends the life of the blocks. Use a 2-inch sand bed, but take extra care that the blocks don't straddle humps or bridge hollows; otherwise, they may crack.

Invisible edgings (see pages 86–87) are generally best with adobe. Railroad ties (shown below) give a more rustic feel.

Laying the blocks. Because their dimensions vary slightly, it's usually difficult to lay adobe blocks in patterns that call for tight fitting. Leave 1-inch open joints between units and scoop out or fill in sand as necessary to compensate for size irregularities. Use a level as you work.

Running bond, jack-on-jack, and basket weave patterns all work well (see page 90); the latter two don't require cutting. If you need to cut adobe, however, it's easy to do with a hammer and brickset (see page 93), or with an old saw.

Filling the joints. The best method is to fill the joints with sand or soil. Because the blocks are so heavy, they'll stay in place without a problem. Filling with soil permits crevice planting, which adds charm.

If you like the clean look of mortared joints, prepare a 1:3 cement-sand mixture, adding 1½ gallons of asphalt stabilizer per bag of cement as a water seal. Apply the mortar as for bricks in wet mortar (see pages 96–97). But use mortar only when it's essential: manufacturers have found that adobe failure often starts at mortar joints.

Setting Adobe in a Sand Bed

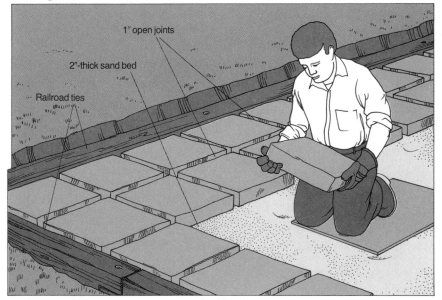

After positioning edgings, lay a 2-inch sand bed. Place blocks about 1 inch apart in a simple pattern, such as running bond, jack-on-jack, or basket weave. Check level as you go, scooping out or adding sand as required.

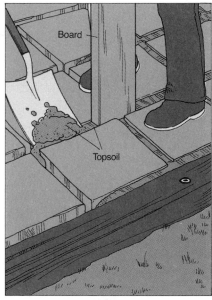

Topsoil and plantings create natural, stabilizing fillers between blocks; board helps pack soil tightly in place.

STONE

Natural stone—cut flagstone, rough cobbles, and the like—looks pleasant in almost any garden setting. Its natural, unfinished appearance blends well with garden plants, and its subdued color lends warmth.

Stone's primary drawback is that it can cost up to five times as much as brick or concrete. Geography often dictates cost: the farther you are from the quarry, the higher the price.

Irregularly shaped flagstones can be laid in firm soil, in a sand bed, or in mortar (over either sand or concrete). Flagstones are also available precut to rectangular shapes; these tighter-fitting pieces work well laid in a bed of sand.

River rock and fieldstone are less expensive, more rustic alternatives to flagstone. Depending on the size of the stones and the effect desired, you can either "seed" them into concrete or place them individually in mortar or in a concrete setting bed.

Working with Flagstone

Since flagstones are typically irregularly shaped, you'll need to fit and cut most pieces before setting them. After preparing the area (see pages 82–84) and adding edgings (see pages 85–87), if appropriate, lay out all the flagstones, shifting them around until you achieve a pleasing design that requires a minimum of cutting.

When a stone requires cutting, let the adjoining one overlap it. Mark the cutting line with a pencil, using the edge of the top stone as a guide.

Score a ⅛-inch-deep groove along the cutting line with a brickset or, for more accuracy, a portable circular saw fitted with a masonry blade. Place a length of wood or an angle iron under the stone so that the waste portion and the scored line overhang it. Strike sharply along the line with a brickset and soft-headed hammer or mallet (protect your eyes).

For smaller trimming jobs, chip off pieces with a mason's hammer. To remove minor surface imperfections, use a sharp brickset and mallet.

Laying Stones in Sand

Stones laid in a bed of sand provide a stable patio surface, especially when the shapes are uniform. The sand helps lock the units together. The technique is the same as for laying bricks in sand (see pages 94–95).

Lay rectangular stones in a tight pattern, bedding each unit with a mallet and checking with a level (see drawing on page 122). Scoop out or fill in sand to compensate for variations in stone thickness.

If you're using irregularly shaped flagstones, the stones should be firmly bedded over their entire surface so they won't wobble when walked on. Pack the joints with soil.

Laying Flagstones in Wet Mortar

For the most permanent flagstone surface, set stones in a mortar bed over at least a 3-inch-thick concrete slab, either existing (clean and in good condition) or new (see pages 100–107—make sure it has cured for at least 24 hours). Ask your concrete dealer whether you need to use a bonding agent on the concrete surface. If the stones are porous, wet them a few hours before setting them.

Setting stones. Before laying the mortar bed, arrange the stones, cutting and trimming them so there's a minimum of space for mortar joints.

Prepare a 1:3 cement-sand mixture, enough to cover 10 to 12 square feet, adding water slowly—the mortar should be stiff enough to support the weight of the stones, but not so stiff that you can't work with it.

(Continued on next page)

Fitting & Cutting Flagstone

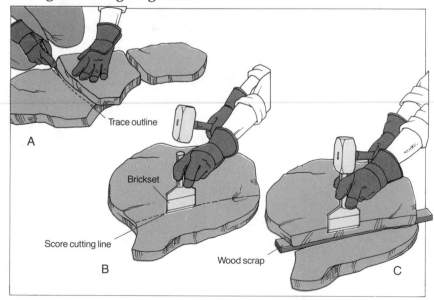

Trace outline

A

Brickset

Score cutting line

B

Wood scrap

C

To custom-fit irregular flagstone, lay one block over its neighbor and trace its outline (A). Then score a ⅛-inch groove in stone to be cut (B). Finally, prop up stone and split with a sharp blow (C).

Setting Rectangular Stones on a Sand Bed

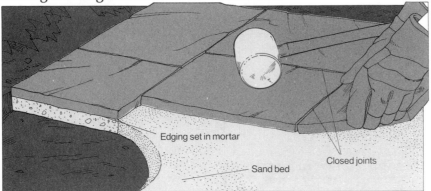

Install invisible edgings in mortar; then screed a 1- to 1½-inch sand bed. Lay flagstones in your chosen pattern with closed or slightly spaced joints, sweeping additional dry sand into joints to lock units together.

Grouting joints. When the mortar has set for 24 hours, pack the joints with the same mortar mix used for the bed—plus an optional ½ to 1 part fireclay to improve workability—and smooth them with a trowel or jointer. Clean the stones as you work.

Keep the grout damp for the first day by sprinkling repeatedly with water or by covering with plastic sheeting. Keep off the paved area for 3 days.

STONE

Starting at one corner, remove a section of stones and set them aside in the same relative positions. With a trowel, spread enough mortar (at least 1 inch deep for the thickest stones) to make a full bed for one or two stones. Furrow the mortar with your trowel. Set each stone firmly in place, bedding it with a rubber mallet.

To maintain an even surface, use a straightedge and level. If a stone isn't level, lift it up and scoop out or add mortar as needed. Clean the stones as you work.

Align the edges of the outer stones with the perimeter of the slab or let them overhang it slightly. Remove any excess mortar from the perimeter.

Laying Pebbles or Cobbles

The appropriate method for setting pebbles or cobbles depends on the size and shape of the stones and the desired effect. Flattened stones 6 inches or more in diameter can be set directly in the soil for a natural look. Smaller cobbles, river stones, or pebbles should be set in mortar or "seeded" into concrete. The latter method requires edgings.

Setting Flagstones in Mortar

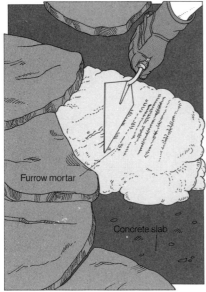

After dry-fitting stones, spread a bed for one or two stones at a time, furrowing mortar with a trowel.

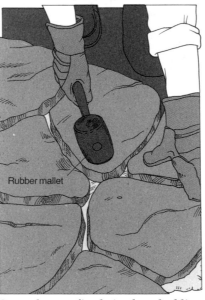

Set each stone firmly in place, bedding it with a rubber mallet and checking for level. Clean stones as you work.

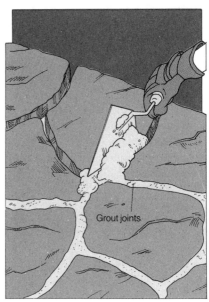

When mortar has set for 24 hours, grout joints and smooth with a trowel.

Creating a Mosaic

Setting mosaics in mortar. You can set decorative pebbles on an existing slab that's clean and in good condition or on a new one (see pages 100–107—leave the surface rough and let the concrete cure for at least 24 hours).

Prepare a 1:3 cement-sand mortar mixture and spread it over the slab to a depth of ½ inch. Stones should be set in the mortar within 2 hours, so spread only as much mortar as you can fill within that time; cut the dry edges away from the previous mortar bed before spreading the next section. Keep the stones in a pail of clean water, setting them in the mortar while they're still wet.

When pressing the stones into the mortar, push them in deep enough so the mortar gets a good "hold" on the edge of the stone—generally just past the middle. Use a board to keep the stones level. Let the mortar set for 2 to 3 hours; then spread a thin layer of mortar over the surface and into the voids. Hose and brush the excess away before it sets.

Labels: ½"-thick mortar bed · Decorative pebbles

Set decorative pebbles in a ½-inch mortar bed over a concrete slab. Spread mortar in small, workable sections; push wet stones into setting bed.

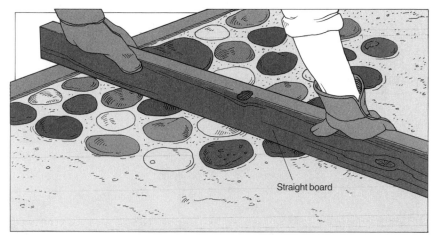

Label: Straight board

Level stones with a straight board, as shown. After 2 to 3 hours, spread a thin layer of mortar over surface; hose and brush excess away.

Setting stones in wet concrete. Stones can be set directly in concrete in two ways. The first, generally used only with small pebbles, is to "seed" them, pressing the stones beneath the surface of the wet concrete and exposing them later. The second method, used for both aggregate and larger stones, is to set them one by one in wet concrete and leave them exposed.

To seed pebbles, build forms, pour the concrete, and level the surface (for concrete techniques, turn to pages 100–107); then follow the instructions for seeding aggregates on pages 107–108.

For larger stones, pour the slab as above, but don't fill the forms completely. Push the stones into the concrete one by one, covering slightly more than half the stone. When the concrete has hardened somewhat, expose the stones as desired by carefully brushing the concrete while wetting down the surface with a fine spray.

Placing Fieldstones in Concrete

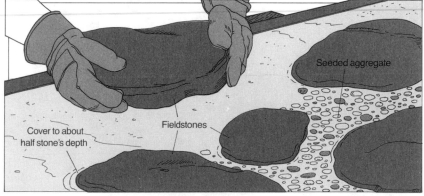

Labels: Cover to about half stone's depth · Fieldstones · Seeded aggregate

To set stones in wet concrete, strike concrete off below tops of forms and push stones in slightly more than halfway. When concrete begins to harden, expose stones by brushing while wetting down surface with a fine spray.

BUILDING PLANTERS

It's easy to find containers for your patio plants. But suppose you want to build your own? Shown below are designs for four planters, plus a hanging post; build them from redwood or another decay-resistant material.

The modular planters are simple to build; they're basically just boxes with butted joints, built in multiples of 8 inches. The interlocking planter is a handsome variation on the basic box; though dimensions are indicated, you can make it any size you wish.

The ridged and 12-sided planters are more ambitious, though not too difficult for a home woodworker armed with a table saw. The trick to cutting the trapezoids is to construct a jig for repetitive cuts at a 30° angle to the saw blade. Once the pieces are cut, it's a matter of clamping, gluing, and nailing them into a finished ring, and then building up the layers.

Bases for all these planters are 1 by 6s or 1 by 8s; drill at least three ¾-inch holes for drainage. Finish your project with clear water seal, wood stain, or diluted enamel. For mobility, you can fasten a set of heavy-duty casters to the base of your planter.

Out of patio space? Our fifth project, the plant post with crossarms, will secure as many as four hanging pots.

A Collection of Planter Projects

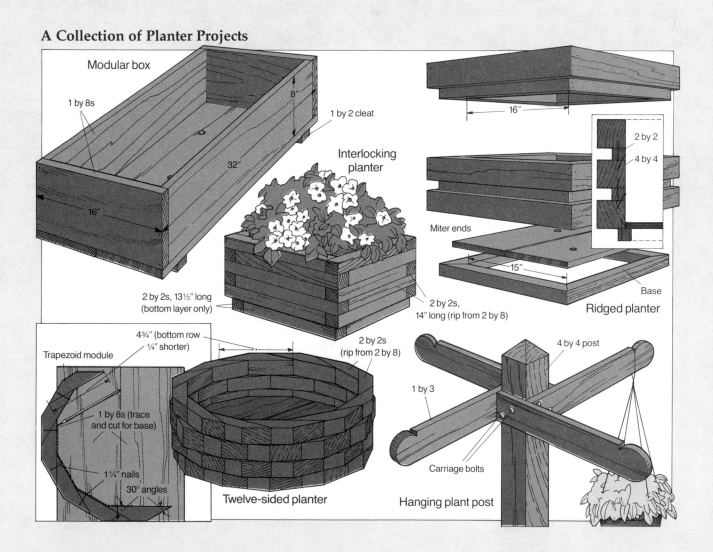

Modular box
1 by 8s
8"
32"
16"
1 by 2 cleat

Interlocking planter
2 by 2s, 13½" long (bottom layer only)

16"
2 by 2
4 by 4
Miter ends
15"
Base
Ridged planter
2 by 2s, 14" long (rip from 2 by 8)

4¾" (bottom row ¼" shorter)
Trapezoid module
1 by 8s (trace and cut for base)
1¼" nails
30° angles
Twelve-sided planter
2 by 2s (rip from 2 by 8)

4 by 4 post
1 by 3
Carriage bolts
Hanging plant post

WOOD

Few materials can match the natural, informal quality of wood. Its warm color and soft texture bring something of the forest into your garden.

Wood rounds, blocks, and timbers are user-friendly materials that give the builder a good deal of freedom in application and construction techniques. But wood rounds and blocks, usually set in place so that the end grain is in contact with the soil, soak up ground moisture; the wood eventually either rots away or succumbs to insect invasion.

For this reason, it's best to choose rot- and insect-resistant heartwood of cedar, redwood, or cypress. Or use wood that's been pressure-treated with preservatives.

Soil or drainage problems that would make wood rounds, concrete, or bricks difficult to install can be overcome with a low-level deck. Because decking is raised above the ground and dries out quickly, it will survive longer under adverse weather conditions.

Preparing the Site

In general, wood paving units require a carefully prepared site. Grade the area as described on pages 82–84. To protect the wood from excessive ground moisture, put down a layer of filter fabric before laying the sand or gravel bed or the wood paving units.

Wood Rounds

Constructing a simple paving made of wood rounds is an easy job.

Put down a 2-inch-thick sand bed. Arrange the rounds on top in a pattern that both fills the area and produces a pleasing design. Make sure the tops are flush with the surface of the ground. Fill the spaces between the rounds with bark, gravel, or large pebbles, or add soil and plant grass or a ground cover.

End-grain Blocks

Wood blocks—cross-sections sawn from 4 by 4 or larger lumber—can be laid in much the same manner as bricks.

When you grade, dig down 1 inch deeper than the thickness of the blocks. Build wood edgings (see pages 85–86), placing the stakes on the outside. Then lay down a 1-inch-thick sand bed. Set the blocks as for bricks in sand (see pages 94–95); then sweep sand into the joints.

This method also works for 1 by 12s or 2 by 12s cut square and laid face up in the sand. Grooves, or dadoes, cut down the center of each board with a router or table saw give the appearance of brick basket weave, as shown below, bottom left.

Railroad Ties

Because they blend well with other patio materials, railroad ties make an effective surface in a limited area. Using them for a large project could prove costly, however, since the ties are expensive.

To set ties flush with the surface, prepare the site as described at left. Either set the ties on a layer of filter fabric or in a sand bed laid over the fabric.

(Continued on next page)

Easy Wood Pavings

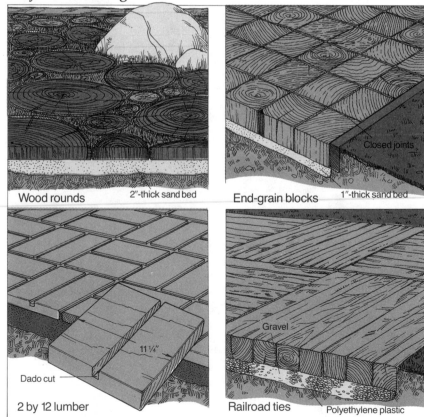

Wood rounds   2"-thick sand bed

End-grain blocks   1"-thick sand bed   Closed joints

Dado cut   11¼"   2 by 12 lumber

Gravel   Railroad ties   Polyethylene plastic

For a raised paving, simply level the site and arrange the ties directly on the ground.

Sleeper Construction

A raised wood "floor" is a particularly good choice where drainage is a problem. Moreover, it adds to the longevity of your patio.

Build a support system from 4 by 4s laid at 24-inch intervals either on tamped earth or on a bed of sand. Using galvanized nails or drywall screws, attach 2 by 4 or 2 by 6 decking to the supports, centering board ends over the supports and staggering the joints (see drawing below).

Modular Decking

Like the sleeper-supported decking described above, modular wood flooring avoids potential drainage problems and has the added benefit of being portable.

Build 32-inch-square support frames (as many as you want) from 2 by 4s or 2 by 6s. Using galvanized nails, attach nine 32-inch 2 by 4s, as shown below, at bottom. Omit a square here or there to accommodate a container plant.

Low-level Decks

A low-level deck—either freestanding or house-attached—provides a solid, relatively durable surface requiring little or no grading and a minimum of maintenance. Such a deck is relatively easy to build (see facing page).

For an attached deck, first lag-screw or bolt a ledger to the house framing—either a rim joist or wall studs.

Dig holes no more than 3½ feet apart for concrete footings, spacing the rows about 5 feet apart. Pour the footings and set in precast concrete piers.

Lay 4 by 4 beams on the piers, using short lengths of 4 by 4 posts as necessary to gain the correct height. Level the beams by inserting shingles or other wood scraps between the beams and the posts or piers. Attach the beams using framing connectors, as shown, or toenail them to the piers. Joints between beams should meet over piers; secure the joints with metal plates or wooden braces.

If the deck is attached to the house, connect the beams to the ledger; typically, beams sit in joist hangers nailed to the ledger.

Then add decking boards—flat 2 by 4s, 2 by 6s, varied widths of 2-by lumber, or other sizes laid on edge. Space the boards ⅛ to 3/16 inch apart to allow for drainage (a 16d nail makes a good spacer) and secure them with galvanized nails or deck screws at least twice as long as the decking's thickness. Trim deck edges as shown.

For more information on building decks, consult a professional.

Two Wood "Floor" Designs

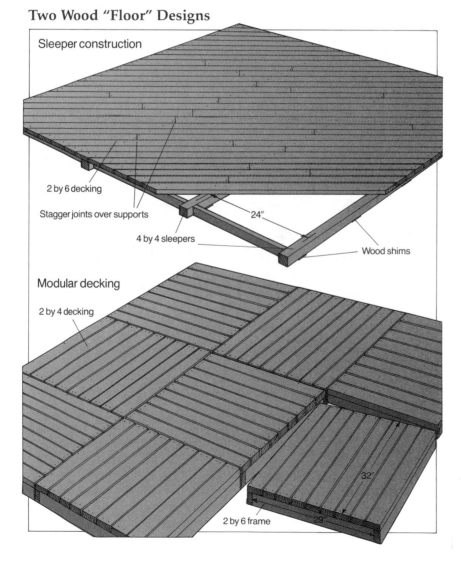

Sleeper construction

2 by 6 decking

Stagger joints over supports

4 by 4 sleepers

24"

Wood shims

Modular decking

2 by 4 decking

2 by 6 frame

32"

29"

Building a Low-level Deck

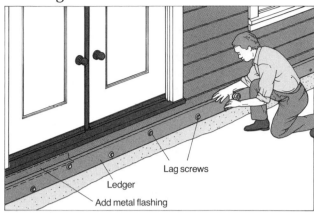

House-attached decks begin with a ledger: after laying out perimeter lines, screw or bolt ledger to house framing. Flash ledger/house seam as shown.

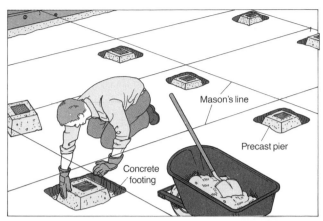

Dig holes for footings, pour concrete, and set precast piers in place; align them carefully with mason's lines, then level tops in both directions.

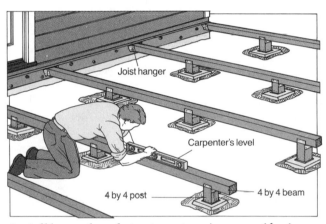

Install beams for substructure atop piers or on 4 by 4 posts cut to correct height. Use shims to make fine adjustments in level.

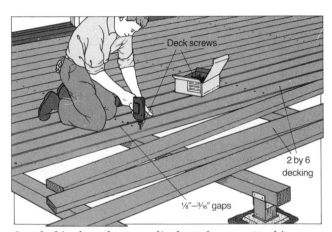

Lay decking boards perpendicular to beams, attaching them at each support; leave gaps between boards for drainage and expansion.

Trim ends of decking boards all at once, using a portable circular saw; a chalk line or long, straight board helps guide cuts.

Finally, nail or screw rim joists across beam ends and trimmed decking boards, mitering ends where pieces meet.

LOOSE MATERIALS

Pea gravel, gorilla hair, redrock: these are just a few of the loose, or soft, materials available for pavings. They blend well with concrete pavers and pads, wood rounds and decking modules, or native stones and boulders. All are sold by the cubic yard or by the ton.

The ideal loose paving material stays where it's laid, drains well so it can be walked on when wet, and keeps shoes free of dust and mud. But loose paving does have some drawbacks: it's slow and uncomfortable for walking, it allows weeds to grow through it, and it must be replenished from time to time.

Preparing the Site

Careful preparation is the key to a first-rate job. To begin, prepare the area to be paved (see pages 82–84), taking into account the recommended depth for the material you're using.

Then install wood or masonry edgings (see pages 85–87) to keep the loose material in bounds. For large areas, consider using a grid of 2 by 4 dividers (built the same way as wood edgings) to help keep the paving more uniformly distributed.

Place sheets of filter fabric or polyethylene plastic on the ground before laying the paving. The lining provides an effective bedding and helps deter the growth of weeds. Puncture the plastic every square foot or so to allow for drainage.

Gravel

Gravel—either smooth river rock or more angular crushed material—provides a low-cost, fast-draining surface; it's particularly effective when used in low-traffic areas, or in combination with smoother, tougher masonry units or poured concrete. The selection of gravel colors, textures, and sizes varies

from region to region; for a sampling, see pages 26–27.

Gravel surfaces tend to "travel" when walked on; this can be minimized by using a compacted base of crushed rock or sand.

Once installed, gravel requires little care. Determined weeds can be pulled or cut away. Pea gravel can be raked to remove leaves or maintain desired patterns; clean larger gravels with a leaf blower or vacuum. You may need to renew heavily trodden surfaces every few years.

Arrange to have the gravel delivered, along with a base material of decomposed granite or construction sand (both should be available from your supplier). If the materials are brought by dump truck and access is available, ask the driver to tailgate-spread them over the area, rather than dump them in one big heap in your driveway.

If you don't already have them, you'll need to rent a wheelbarrow and

Laying Down Gravel

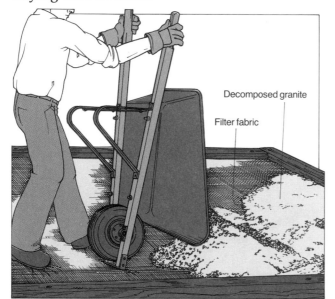

After installing edgings, put down filter fabric or plastic sheeting for weed protection. Then lay down decomposed granite or sand.

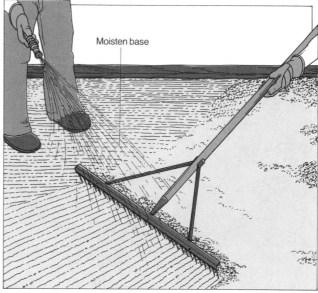

Rake out base material evenly over the site, forming a uniform 1-inch thickness; wet base down with a hose as you rake.

an iron rake for hauling and spreading, and a large drum roller (shown below) to pack both the base and the gravel.

Laying the base. Spread a 1-inch-thick layer of granite or sand over the site, distributing it evenly with a rake; then wet the base. Roll it several times with a drum roller to pack it firmly.

Adding gravel. Spread gravel 2 to 3 inches thick. (Coverage varies with size and weight, but generally, you'll need 1 ton of rock to cover 100 square feet.) Using the roller, compress the gravel into place (rolling also helps turn sharp edges down).

Adding stepping-stones. An excellent way to make a gravel patio more stable is to add stepping-stones—either thick flagstones or concrete pavers. Place the stepping-stones on packed base material so that their tops will be slightly above the surrounding gravel.

Bark

Bark, a by-product of the lumber industry, is available in a variety of sizes. Choose the one that gives the effect you want.

Lay bark 2 to 4 inches thick on the prepared base. Gorilla hair—finely shredded redwood bark—makes a natural-looking, springy top dressing. Add it to the bark base. Or use it atop decomposed granite or crushed rock (see below).

Decomposed Granite & Crushed Rock

Because particle sizes range from sand to quite large pieces of rock, decomposed granite and crushed rock make good pavings that pack tightly together and don't move underfoot.

Lay these materials over the prepared site in the same way as for the decomposed granite base for gravel (see at left). In this case, however, plan to build up a 2½- to 4-inch-thick paving in 1-inch increments.

Redrock

Redrock—a mixture of clay, sand, and soil—compacts well when damp, but it does break down, becoming dusty in time, so you'll have to add new material periodically.

Because redrock isn't always graded by size, you may need a ¼-inch mesh sieve to sift out enough fine material to set aside for a ¾-inch-thick topping.

After preparing the base, lay and level a 2½- to 4-inch-thick layer of the larger material, building it up in 1-inch increments, wetting it down, and rolling it with a drum roller. Finally, distribute the sifted material evenly over the base, dampening and rolling once more.

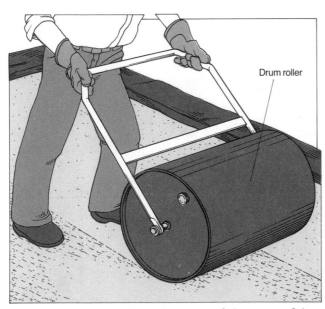

Using a drum roller, roll wet base several times to pack it evenly. A firm base helps keep gravel topcoat from "traveling" underfoot.

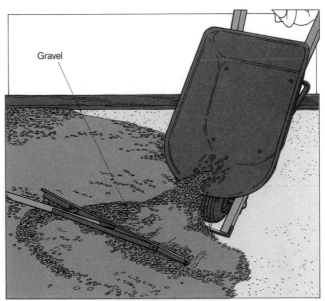

Finally, spread gravel 2 to 3 inches thick and rake evenly over base. Roll several times, compressing gravel and locking it into place.

BUILDING PATIO BENCHES

Although commercial benches and seats are readily available, designing and building your own allows you to have patio seating that blends with your landscaping and is exactly right for you.

Bench Design

For comfort, a seat should be 15 to 18 inches high, the approximate height of most chairs. If you plan to use a thick cushion, build the seat lower. Make it lower still—12 inches or less from the ground—if you intend to use it primarily for sunbathing.

There's no set guide for depth. A bench only 12 inches deep looks more like a place to perch than a place to relax. A depth of 15 to 18 inches is comfortable for sitting. For lounging, you can make the bench even deeper—24 inches is the width of a standard lounge pad.

Legs should be sturdy enough for solid support and still be in scale with the rest of the bench. Space them about 3 to 5 feet apart if they're made of 4 by

4s. If you're using a lighter-weight material, place the legs closer together. Be sure to plan for a kick-space beneath the seat.

Bench Materials

Redwood, pine, cedar, fir, and cypress are the woods most frequently used for outdoor seating. If the legs will be in contact with the ground, choose the heartwood of redwood, cedar, or cypress, or use pressure-treated lumber.

For a sturdy seat, select top-quality lumber 2 inches thick and without loose knots. You can also make the seat of 1 by 2s or 1 by 3s set on edge. To prevent unsightly staining, use only galvanized nails, screws, and bolts.

Building Tips

Prebore holes for screws and bolts, and countersink them so the heads don't extend above the surface, where they can snag clothing. If you're using nails, predrilling the holes will reduce the chance of the wood's splitting. Set the nail heads with a nailset.

Once the seat is built, sand or plane all exposed wood surfaces smooth and round off the edges. You may need to do this periodically to keep the surfaces smooth and free of splinters.

Either leave the wood natural, allowing it to weather, or apply sealer, stain, or paint.

Bench Basics

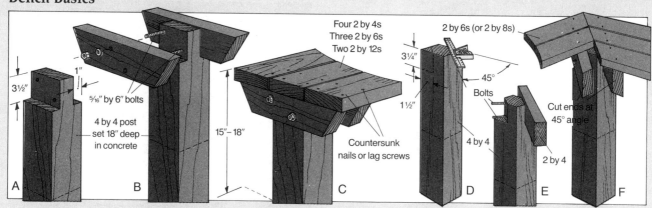

For a simple bench, saw shoulders in 4 by 4 posts (A) and set in place; then bolt 2 by 4 braces to posts (B) and nail on planks (C). For a corner bench, mark posts as shown (D), saw shoulders and add braces (E), and then nail on mitered planks (F).

Bench Designs

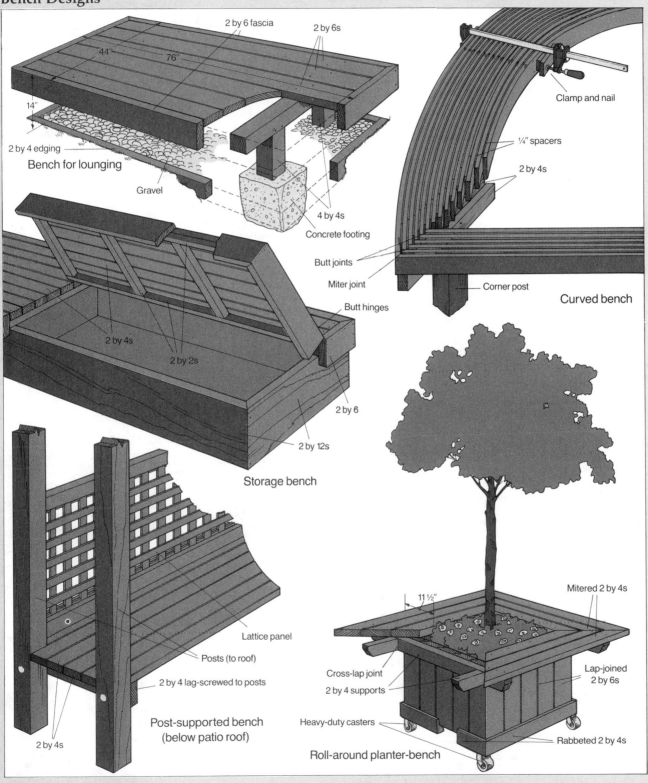

Bench for lounging
- 2 by 6 fascia
- 2 by 6s
- 44"
- 76"
- 14"
- 2 by 4 edging
- Gravel
- 4 by 4s
- Concrete footing

Curved bench
- Clamp and nail
- ¼" spacers
- 2 by 4s
- Butt joints
- Miter joint
- Corner post

Storage bench
- 2 by 4s
- 2 by 2s
- Butt hinges
- 2 by 6
- 2 by 12s

Post-supported bench (below patio roof)
- Lattice panel
- Posts (to roof)
- 2 by 4 lag-screwed to posts
- 2 by 4s

Roll-around planter-bench
- 11½"
- Mitered 2 by 4s
- Cross-lap joint
- 2 by 4 supports
- Heavy-duty casters
- Lap-joined 2 by 6s
- Rabbeted 2 by 4s

RETAINING WALLS

If your house sits on a sloping lot, you may need to include a retaining wall in your patio plan. Building most kinds of retaining walls is demanding work. High walls especially have to be sturdy and well designed because of the enormous weight of the soil they hold back.

Most localities require a building permit for any retaining wall. Many require that a licensed engineer design and supervise the construction of any retaining wall over 3 feet high or one on an unstable or steep slope.

Hardy, firm-rooted plants that cover well but won't spread too quickly can help hold the soil behind the wall. Plant immediately after completing the wall, while the soil is still soft and easily worked.

Location & Drainage

If space permits, the safest way to build a retaining wall is to locate it at the bottom of a gentle slope and fill in behind it with soil. Or the hill can be held with a series of low walls that form terraces, or with a single high wall. All three methods are shown on page 73. Notice that in each case the retaining wall rests on cut or undisturbed ground, never on fill. If extensive grading is required, it's best to hire a professional.

Retaining walls must have adequate drainage to prevent water from building up behind them. Surface water can be collected in a shallow ditch dug along the top of the wall. Subsurface water can be collected in a gravel backfill and channeled away either through a drainpipe buried behind the wall or through weep holes evenly spaced along the wall at ground level. (Weep holes may require a ditch along the base of the wall to prevent water from spilling onto the patio.)

Make sure all drainpipes and ditches are properly sloped so they direct the excess water to an appropriate disposal site.

Designs for Retaining Walls

A variety of materials can be used for retaining walls, though engineering must take precedence over appearance in most cases.

Wood. You can make retaining walls in various sizes from boards or from railroad ties set vertically or horizontally. Use heartwood of redwood, cedar, or cypress, or pressure-treated lumber.

To build a 2-foot-high board wall like that shown below, at left, set posts in concrete, spacing them closely and sinking up to half their length into the ground as required by your building code. Nail the boards to the upslope side of the posts and line them with moisture-proof building paper. In the gravel behind the wall, install 4-inch perforated drainpipe. A cap of 2 by 6s strengthens the wall and acts as a garden seat.

Retaining Walls in Profile

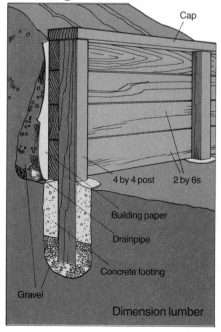

Cap

4 by 4 post   2 by 6s

Building paper

Drainpipe

Concrete footing

Gravel

Dimension lumber

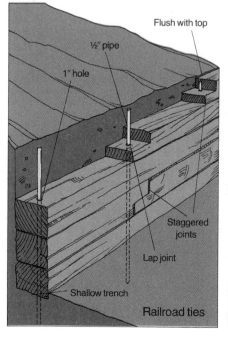

Flush with top

½" pipe

1" hole

Staggered joints

Lap joint

Shallow trench

Railroad ties

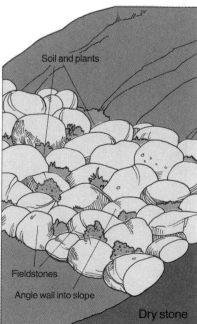

Soil and plants

Fieldstones

Angle wall into slope

Dry stone

Railroad ties are popular because of their bold, rugged look, but they're hard to lift, drill, and cut. To set ties horizontally for a low wall, place them in a shallow trench of hard-tamped earth. Then stack ties, staggering their joints and toenailing them to each other with long galvanized spikes. Use pipes or reinforcing rods to reinforce the walls; or bolt the ties to 4 by 4 posts.

To set ties vertically for a straight or curved wall, soak the cut ends in wood preservative. Set them in the soil so half their length is above the ground. For stability, you can set the ends in concrete and connect the ties along the back with a continuous strip of sheet metal, such as flashing, fastened with wide-headed nails.

Dry walls. A stone or broken-concrete retaining wall laid without mortar is a good choice for a low, fairly stable slope. The crevices between the rocks or concrete are ideal for colorful plantings.

Heavy, uncut stone requires patience to lay. Fit the stones carefully (their uneven surfaces will help hold them in place), laying them so they tip back into the slope. Set soil in pockets between the rocks as you build.

Use a sledgehammer to break concrete into pieces. Lay the rubble, smooth sides down, in courses, staggering the joints.

Unit masonry walls. Walls built of masonry units mortared together are good for holding steep or unstable hillsides.

Brick, adobe, and stone are suitable materials for low mortared walls. Ask your building department about requirements for reinforcing. For building help, turn to the appropriate sections in this chapter or consult a professional mason.

For a high wall, concrete blocks are best. The block wall shown below, at left, rests on a footing reinforced with steel rods. The wall itself is built of bond-beam blocks, with horizontal re-

inforcing as needed. Grouting is done by courses. Drainpipes form weep holes for drainage. Capping the wall with mortar and applying a brick or stone veneer make the wall more attractive.

Poured concrete walls. A poured concrete wall reinforced with steel is the strongest type of retaining wall. However, both the formwork and the labor make it a very costly project.

Poured concrete walls can be either mass walls or cantilevered. A mass wall, such as the one shown below, relies on its own weight to prevent it from tipping or sliding. The width of the base must be half to three-quarters of the wall's height. On low walls, steel reinforcing isn't usually required, but a horizontal ⅜-inch rod near the top adds strength.

Cantilevered poured concrete walls, like concrete-block walls, rely on the weight of the earth pressing down on a large footing to hold them in place.

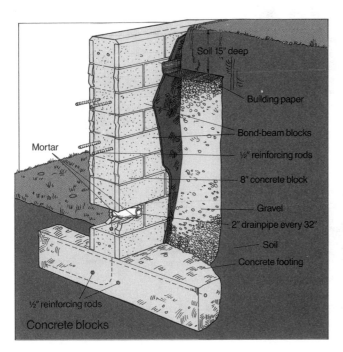

Soil 15" deep
Building paper
Bond-beam blocks
½" reinforcing rods
8" concrete block
Gravel
2" drainpipe every 32"
Soil
Concrete footing
Mortar
½" reinforcing rods
Concrete blocks

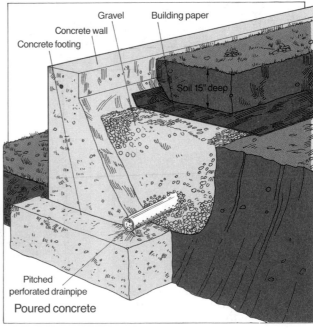

Gravel
Building paper
Concrete wall
Concrete footing
Soil 15" deep
Pitched perforated drainpipe
Poured concrete

RAISED BEDS

A well-designed raised planting bed provides a smooth transition between levels and, as an added advantage, puts plants at a more convenient height. In some cases, the restrictions governing retaining walls may also apply to raised beds; however, most planters are no more than 12 to 18 inches high.

Materials

Any of the materials suited for retaining walls (see pages 132–133) can be used for raised beds. Wood, brick, stone, and concrete are all prime candidates, depending on your overall landscaping scheme.

Wood is especially versatile, as the drawing on the facing page shows. Railroad ties and other large timbers, though somewhat awkward to handle, make attractive, rustic walls for raised beds. Unadorned wood planks and stakes complement nearly any landscape design and are easily adapted to various shapes and sizes.

Building a Low Brick Wall

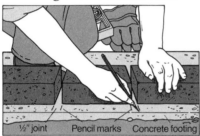

Lay a dry course of bricks along a line marking wall's edge. Allow ½ inch for joints, marking footing with a pencil.

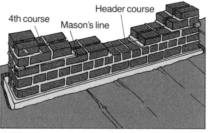

Lay first three bricks on a mortar bed, level, and then tap into place with trowel handle. Add a backup course.

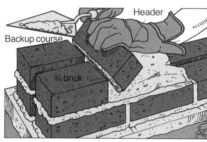

Begin header course by cutting two ¾ bricks and mortaring them in place. Then mortar four headers across wall.

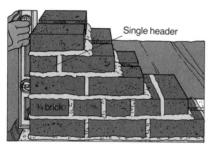

Finish lead with stretchers (header begins fourth row) until it's four courses high. Build lead at other end.

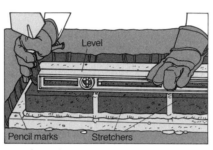

Fill in between leads, keeping mason's line flush with top of course being laid. Lay bricks from ends toward center.

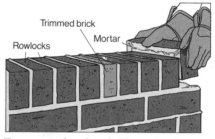

To cap, use headers laid on edge (row-locks). Mortar top course and bricks; set cut brick in from end.

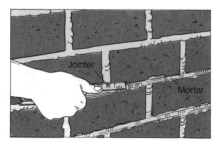

Run jointer along thumbprint-hard mortar to compact and smooth. (Do horizontal joints first.)

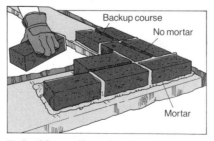

To build a wall with corners, square layout; then build up corner leads. Lay corner bricks first; then add backup.

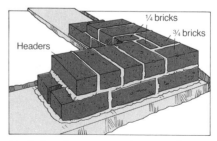

Begin header course using ¼ and ¾ bricks at corner; complete lead course. Finish wall between leads.

Whatever design you choose, always remember to use pressure-treated lumber or the decay-resistant heartwood of cedar, redwood, or cypress.

Raised beds made of unit masonry are strong and enduring, and can be constructed in many different shapes and styles. A planting bed made of brick (see drawings on facing page) can lend elegance and distinction to a formal garden scheme. Even a plain concrete block wall can be dressed up with a veneer of stone or brick. Poured concrete or broken pieces of old concrete from former pavings also work well for raised beds.

Construction

Raised beds are usually easy to build. The vertical supporting face acts like a small retaining wall, with one significant difference: a raised bed rarely has to withstand the soil pressure that's exerted on most retaining walls.

Drainage is most important. If the bed is open at the bottom, most excess water will drain out. If it's closed, make weep holes 2 to 3 inches from the ground, spaced 2 to 3 feet apart. Place a 4-inch layer of crushed rock in the bed before filling it with soil.

Tree Walls & Wells

When you need to sharply lower the soil level around a mature tree, a raised bed retains the soil under the tree at its original level.

If the ground level needs to be raised, build a wall around the tree before grading. Pile soil up against it, making the wall the outside of a well.

Build the tree wall or well of stone, concrete, brick, or wood. Locate the wall at the drip line under the tree's outermost branches. (The branches mirror the underground root structure, enabling you to determine where the roots lie.)

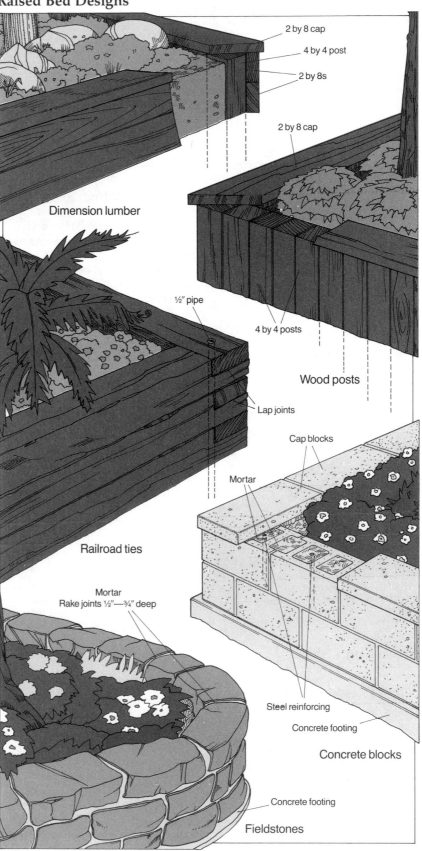

Raised Bed Designs

2 by 8 cap
4 by 4 post
2 by 8s
2 by 8 cap

Dimension lumber

2 by 8 cap

½" pipe

4 by 4 posts

Wood posts

Lap joints

Cap blocks

Mortar

Railroad ties

Mortar
Rake joints ½"—¾" deep

Steel reinforcing

Concrete footing

Concrete blocks

Concrete footing

Fieldstones

GARDEN STEPS

Changes of level in your patio or garden may call for just a few steps or an entire flight. Well-designed steps begin with an understanding of proper step proportions. Poured concrete (with mortared masonry units, if desired), railroad ties, and dimension lumber are all appropriate materials for steps.

Design Principles

To design steps, you must determine the proportions of the steps and the degree of the slope.

Step Proportions

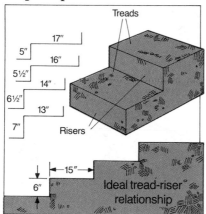

Tread-to-riser ratio remains constant, even as dimensions vary.

Measuring a Slope

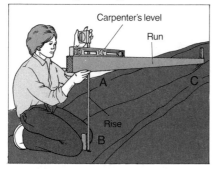

Simple device measures rise (height) and run (length) of slope.

Proportions. The flat surface of a step is called the tread; the vertical surface is the riser. Ideally, the depth of the tread plus twice the riser height should equal 25 to 27 inches. For both safety and ease of walking, the ideal dimensions are a 6-inch-high riser with a 15-inch-deep tread.

As the chart at left shows, riser and tread dimensions can vary, but the riser-tread relationship remains the same. Risers should be no lower than 5 inches and no higher than 8 inches. Tread depth should never be less than 11 inches. And all the risers and treads in any one flight of steps should be uniform in size.

Dimensions. Using the drawing at bottom left as a guide, calculate the distance from A to B; this is the rise, or change in level, of your slope. The distance from A to C is the run, the minimum length your steps will run.

To determine the number of steps you'll need, divide the desired riser height into the total rise of the slope. If the answer ends in a fraction (as it probably will), drop the fraction and divide the whole number into the vertical distance; the resulting figure will give you the exact measurement for each of your risers.

Plan on a minimum width of 2 feet for simple utility steps. For main steps, 4 feet is a good minimum width—and make that 5 feet if you want two people to be able to walk abreast.

Fitting the terrain. Rarely will the steps fit exactly into a slope as it is. Plan to cut and fill the slope, as shown on page 73, to accommodate the steps.

If your slope is too steep even for 8-inch risers, remember that steps need not run straight up and down. Some of the most attractive and easily traversed steps curve or zigzag their way up a slope. These create a longer walking distance between levels, but make the slope gentler.

Concrete Steps

Steps can be built entirely of concrete, or the concrete can be used as a base for mortared masonry units.

Preparing the base and building forms. First, form rough steps in the earth, keeping the treads as level and the risers as perpendicular as possible. Allow space for at least a 6-inch gravel setting bed and at least a 4-inch thickness of concrete on both treads and risers. (In severe climates, you may need 6 to 8 inches of concrete, plus a deeper footing below the frost line.) Tamp any filled areas thoroughly, substituting coarse (¾-inch and larger) aggregate for earth where possible.

Using 2-inch-thick lumber, build forms similar to the wood edgings described on page 85. Level and nail the forms to stakes driven into the ground on the outside of the forms so you can remove them later.

Lay the gravel bed, keeping it 4 inches back from the front of the steps as shown on page 103; this way, the concrete will be extra thick at that potentially weak point. To reinforce, add 6-inch-square welded mesh as for concrete paving.

Pouring and finishing. Pour and screed the concrete as for a poured concrete paving. For less slippery treads, roughen them by brooming the surface. Cure as for paving.

If your plans call for installing bricks, pavers, or other masonry units in a mortar bed over the concrete, follow the steps for patio pavings of the appropriate material.

Railroad-tie Steps

Railroad ties make simple, rugged steps. Installation is relatively easy, but because each tie weighs about 150 pounds, you'll almost certainly need a helper.

Excavate the site, tamping the soil in the tread area very firmly.

On firm soil, the ties can be secured with ½-inch galvanized steel pipes or ¾-inch reinforcing rods. Drill a 1-inch hole about a foot from both ends of each tie. Position the ties. Then, using a sledgehammer, drive the pipes or rods through the ties directly into the ground.

For extra support, pour small concrete footings. Set anchor bolts in the slightly stiffened concrete. When the concrete has set (after about 2 days), bolt the ties to the footings.

Once the ties are in place, fill the tread spaces behind them with poured concrete, brick-in-sand paving, or another material of your choice.

Wood Steps

Formal wood steps are best for a low-level deck or for easy access from a house or through a wood retaining wall. Two of the most common types of straight-run wood steps are shown in the drawing at right. Steps with treads supported by wood or metal cleats are easier to build than those with treads cut into stringers.

Make stringers from 2 by 10s or 2 by 12s. (If the steps are more than 4 feet wide, you'll need a third stringer in the middle.)

Use galvanized bolts or metal joist hangers to secure the tops of the stringers to a deck beam or joist, as shown; if you're running stringers off stucco siding or another masonry surface, hang them on a ledger. Note that when bolts are used, the first tread is below the surface of the interior floor or deck; with joist hangers, the first tread must be level with the floor.

Secure the stringers at the bottom to wood nailing blocks anchored in a concrete footing.

Step Design Options

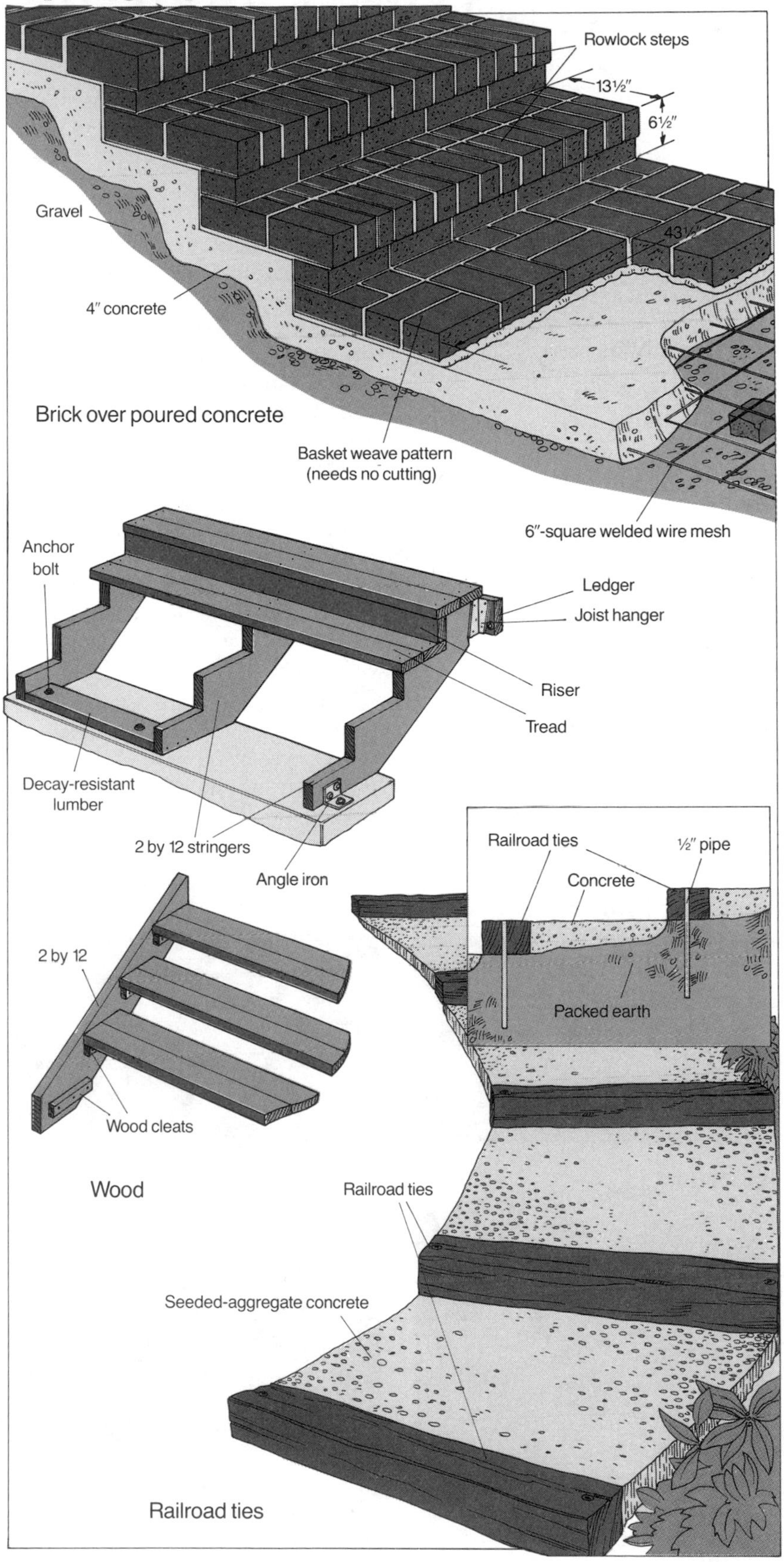

Rowlock steps
13½"
6½"
43½"
Gravel
4" concrete
Basket weave pattern (needs no cutting)
6"-square welded wire mesh

Brick over poured concrete

Anchor bolt
Ledger
Joist hanger
Riser
Tread
Decay-resistant lumber
2 by 12 stringers
Angle iron

2 by 12
Wood cleats

Wood

Railroad ties
½" pipe
Concrete
Packed earth
Railroad ties
Seeded-aggregate concrete

Railroad ties

MAINTENANCE & REPAIR

Although most patio materials are fairly durable and maintenance-free, they occasionally require cleaning and repair.

The following section describes the care and repair of masonry surfaces.

Cleaning Masonry

Most masonry can be kept clean with a simple dousing of water, but you may occasionally have a problem that water can't cure. Here are some problems and their remedies.

Efflorescence. Efflorescence is a white, powdery deposit caused by water dissolving the mineral salts contained in cement and brick. These harmless deposits will disappear after a few years once all the salts have been leached out.

If you prefer not to wait, try brushing and scrubbing the deposits away without using water (water will redissolve some of the salts and carry them back under the surface); then follow with a thorough hosing.

For a stronger cure in extreme cases, follow the directions for removing mortar smears, below.

Mortar smears. A muriatic acid solution removes mortar smears. Available at masonry supply stores, muriatic acid works by attacking the calcium contained in cement and mortar.

Use a 1:9 acid-water solution on concrete, concrete block, and dark brick. On light-colored brick, this solution may leave stains, so use a 1:14 or 1:19 solution. Do not use acid on colored concrete; it may leach out the color. Never use it on stone.

When preparing the solution, always pour the acid *slowly* into the water—*never* the reverse. Wear eye protection and rubber gloves, and work in a well-ventilated area. Using a stiff brush, apply the acid to a small area at a time; let it stand for 3 or 4 minutes and then flush thoroughly with water.

Because muriatic acid can change the color of masonry, you may want to treat the entire area, even though mortar smears or efflorescence affect only one part.

Stains. Ordinary household detergents and cleansers can handle most masonry stains. Some precautions, as well as specific remedies, are discussed below.

Remember that anything strong enough to stain masonry has probably penetrated the surface and may be impossible to remove completely. To prevent stains from occurring in the first place, protect surfaces such as brick barbecue areas with 3 or 4 coats of a commercial sealer (one with a silicone base works best).

The directions below apply only to cleaning concrete and brick. Stone, especially soft sandstone and limestone, cannot be cleaned with acids. Instead, use water only—even detergents can be harmful—and scrub with a fiber brush (steel is too abrasive and may leave rust marks). Sometimes, you can abrade stains on stone by rubbing it with a piece of the same rock.

■ *Oil and grease.* If you catch the stain before it has penetrated, scatter fine sawdust, cement powder, or hydrated lime over the surface. These will soak up much of the oil or grease, and then can be simply swept up.

If the stain has penetrated, try dissolving it with a commercial degreaser or emulsifier (available at masonry and auto supply centers). Follow the manufacturer's directions for use. Residual stains can sometimes be lightened with household bleach (see "Rust," facing page). Avoid hazardous solvents, such as kerosene, benzene, or gasoline; they aren't worth the risks of fire or toxic inhalation.

Removing Mortar Smears

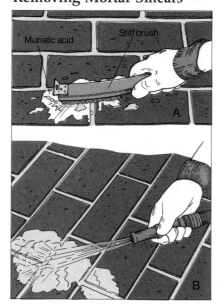

To remove excess mortar, brush on muriatic acid solution (A). Let stand for a few minutes; then flush with water (B).

Renewing Mortar Joints

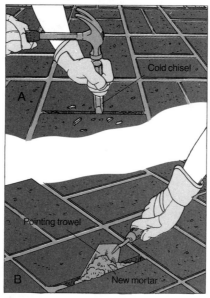

To renew a mortar joint, chisel out old mortar (A); then wet units. Press new mortar into joints (B), tooling it to match.

■ *Paint.* To clean up freshly spilled paint, scrub it with a rag soaked in the solvent specified for the paint. For dried paint, use a commercial paint remover, following the manufacturer's instructions.

■ *Rust.* Ordinary household bleach will lighten rust stains (and most others). Scrub it in, let it stand, and then rinse thoroughly.

For a stronger remedy, mix a pound of oxalic acid into a gallon of water, following the mixing instructions for muriatic acid (see "Mortar smears," facing page). Brush it on, let it stand for 3 or 4 minutes, and then hose it off.

Remember that bleach and acid washes can affect the color of a surface. Test them in an inconspicuous area first.

■ *Smoke and soot.* Using a stiff brush, scrub smoke and soot stains with household scouring powder; then rinse.

Repairing Unit Masonry

Cracked and broken bricks, crumbling mortar joints, and chipped tiles are problems that may never occur in a well-built masonry structure. But shifting earth, impacts, freeze-thaw cycles, and other occurrences beyond human control can damage even the best mason's work.

Most trouble in a mortared pavement develops at the mortar joints. Sometimes, the cement-base mortar commonly used today shrinks, causing the joints to open; old-fashioned lime-base mortar just crumbles.

Freeze-thaw cycles aggravate the problem. Water penetrates the tiniest cracks; when it freezes, it expands, enlarging the cracks and making it more likely that the problem will recur. Renewing the existing mortar joints will eliminate shrinking, crumbling, and cracking.

Settling cracks the joints of a mortared pavement, and sometimes the units themselves. Heavy impacts can result in similar damage. The remedy is to replace the mortar and possibly one or more units. In extreme cases, a whole section of paving may need to be replaced.

Renewing mortar joints. Fresh mortar will not adhere to old, so you'll have to chisel out the old mortar. Use a hammer and narrow-bladed cold chisel (wear eye protection). Expose the joints to a depth of at least ¾ inch; then thoroughly brush and blow the joints out.

Wet the joints with a brush or fine spray. Mix 1:2 cement-sand mortar (see page 93) to a stiff consistency while waiting for the surface moisture to evaporate.

When the units are damp but not wet, use a joint filler or small pointing trowel to press the mortar into the joints. You may find that a hawk—a small mortar board with a handle—will help you keep the mortar close at hand.

Fill the joints completely, tamping the mortar in well (use a small piece of wood for deep joints). Tool the joints when the mortar is stiff enough. Keep the repair damp for 4 days to cure the mortar.

Filling long cracks. You can fill long cracks with mortar, as described above, but grouting is easier.

Wet cracked surfaces with a brush or fine spray. Prepare a 1:2 cement-sand mixture that's thin enough to pour. When surfaces are damp but not wet, pour the grout into the cracks from a bent can; smooth the patch with a damp sponge. Keep the area damp for 4 days to cure the grout.

Replacing individual units. When a unit is badly damaged, you can replace it, provided it carries no load. To replace a unit, chip out the old mortar with a narrow-bladed cold chisel,

Repairing a Crack

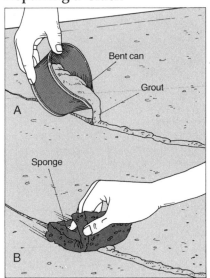

Fill long masonry cracks with grout, pouring it from a bent can (A); smooth surface with damp sponge (B).

Replacing Paving Units

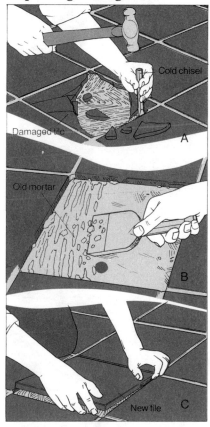

Remove damaged unit (A), scraping out old mortar (B). Apply mortar to cavity and lay new unit (C). Add mortar and tool joints as required.

Fixing a Concrete Crack

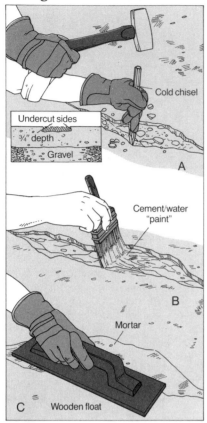

Clean out a large crack as shown (A); coat area with cement/water mix (B) and patch immediately (C).

Mending a Slab

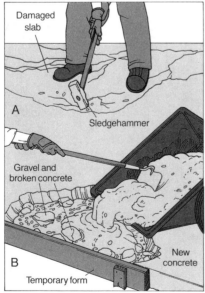

Break up area (A). Add temporary forms as required, fill hole partially with rubble, and pour in concrete (B).

working carefully so as not to disturb adjacent units (wear eye protection). Remove the unit (if necessary, break it up carefully with the chisel and remove the pieces).

Clean the cavity, removing all the old mortar.

Wet the cavity and replacement unit with a brush or fine spray. Mix 1:2 cement-sand mortar to the consistency of soft mud.

When the cavity is damp but not wet, apply a thick layer of mortar to the bottom and sides; then push the new unit into place. Mortar should squeeze from the joints; if not, add more. Remove the excess. Tool the joints and keep the area damp for 4 days to cure the mortar.

Repairing Poured Concrete

Concrete is hard and durable; yet if it's not placed, finished, and cured correctly, flaws can develop. Impacts, shifting earth, and freeze-thaw cycles can also take their toll.

The success of any patch job on concrete depends largely on the care you take in preparing the surface. Always clean all dust and debris from the area to be repaired, and soak it thoroughly, even the previous day, before beginning work. There should be no standing water, but the surface must be damp to ensure a good bond.

In any repair in which the patch will be thin or will need to be feathered at its edges, you'll find the extra strength of commercial latex or epoxy-cement patching compounds well worth their extra cost.

Correcting surface flaws. The most common surface flaws in concrete are dusting, where the surface wears away easily; scaling, where thin layers flake away from the surface; and crazing, where fine networks of surface cracks appear.

■ *To remedy light damage,* clean and soak the area; then apply a 1:1 solution of linseed oil and mineral spirits. The oil will retard further damage and aid in protecting the concrete from deterioration due to the use of de-icing salts. You'll need to renew this coating every few years.

■ *For more severe damage* that requires resurfacing, use either regular Portland cement mortar (a 1:3 cement-sand mixture is good) or, for thin layers, a mortar to which a commercial epoxy or latex-base bonding compound has been added.

Prepare the surface by removing all loose and flaking concrete. A small sledgehammer, used gently, will help break up scaling surfaces. Clean the area and soak it thoroughly.

Mix and apply the mortar, following the directions on page 93, or, for an epoxy or latex-base mixture, follow the manufacturer's instructions. Finish the patch to match the existing surface and cure (see pages 106–107).

Fixing cracks. Using a trowel, fill cracks up to about ⅛ inch wide with a stiff paste of cement and water or with a commercial cement-base caulk.

Clean out larger cracks with a hammer and narrow-bladed cold chisel, working to create a pocket ¾ inch deep or more for the repair material. Undercut the sides, as shown at top left, to provide a positive "lock" for the patching material.

Clean and wet the area; then fill the crack with 1:3 cement-sand mortar mixed to the consistency of soft mud; or use a commercial latex or epoxy-cement patching compound.

To improve the bond, you may want to coat the area first with a thick "paint" of cement and water. Apply the patch immediately—don't let the coating dry. Commercial epoxy bonding compounds, used in the same way, form an even stronger bond.

Finish the patch to match the existing surface and cure.

Mending heavily damaged slabs.
Badly broken concrete slabs should be rebuilt with more concrete. If the damage is extensive, this may mean erecting forms and pouring a new slab (see pages 100–107).

Begin by breaking up the damaged area (for pointers, see pages 88–89); use the pieces as filler in the repair.

If the gravel base has sunk, build it up with more gravel and bits of broken concrete. Clean the edges of the patch area and soak everything thoroughly with water. Wait several hours for the standing water to be absorbed before placing the fresh concrete. If the broken area extends to the slab edge, erect temporary forms (see drawing on bottom of facing page).

Mix a batch of 1:3:3 cement-sand-aggregate sufficient to fill the area; place, finish, and cure it.

If the slab must carry heavy loads, you'll need to add reinforcing, locking the repaired area to the old slab. Drill holes in the exposed edges before adding the new concrete; then cement pieces of reinforcing rod in with mortar or commercial masonry adhesive. Tie welded wire mesh (see page 102) to the rods with wire; support the mesh in the center with bits of broken concrete. Then rebuild as described above.

To give an old, weathered slab a new face, you can float a new 1-inch layer on top. First, roughen up the existing concrete (see drawing at right, top), clean the surface, and soak it down thoroughly. Build forms or edgings up to the new height, then add a thin coat of mortar to act as a bonding agent. Pour and screed the new concrete topcoat and finish as desired.

Asphalt Repairs

Though it's a nettlesome chore that may need repeating every few years, repairing and resealing an asphalt surface will help prolong its life. Oil-base asphalt expands and contracts, an advantage in areas with expansive soils and extreme temperature swings. But asphalt tends to dry out and deteriorate over time, and soil movement or erosion can cause cracking and crumbling.

Before patching or sealing, scrape away any built-up oil and grease; if necessary, scrub with an asphalt driveway solvent, using a stiff brush or broom. Brush dirt and grit off the surface, and hose with a hard spray; let the surface dry.

To patch small potholes, buy ready-to-use loose asphalt. Pour it out, rake it even, and then pack it down, following the manufacturer's instructions. For deep fissures, apply a concentrated filler before spreading with a top coating (see below).

To seal old asphalt, you'll need either a basic coating or a slightly thicker coating-plus-filler. Five gallons of either will cover roughly 400 square feet.

Several grades of both coal-tar and oil-emulsion top coatings are available. More common on hardware store shelves, coal-tar coating dries to a slick surface in about a day and won't track in on your shoes. To find out if you can add sand for better traction, read the label or ask your dealer.

Slowly becoming more available, oil-emulsion coating is the choice of many professionals. Better grades dry in a few days and hold up longer than coal-tar products.

Whichever you choose, pour out a puddle, spread with the bristle side of the long-handled tool shown at right, and smooth with the other side. Cover 3 to 4 square feet at a time, applying a 1/16- to 1/8-inch-thick coating.

Avoid inhaling fumes and keep pets away until the surface is completely dry.

For professional resurfacing contractors, look in the Yellow Pages under "Asphalt & Asphalt Products."

A New Concrete Topcoat

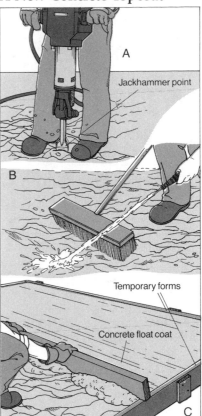

Roughen old slab (A) and scrub and soak (B). Add a thin coat of mortar; then float new concrete (C).

Renewing Asphalt

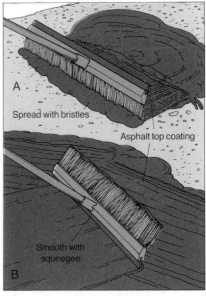

Spread top coating with bristle side of asphalt tool (A); smooth surface with other side (B).

LANDSCAPING WITH WATER

You may be surprised to learn how easy it is to bring the soothing sound and sight of water to your new patio environment. Installing a tub garden is almost as simple as filling a container with some water lilies or perhaps a few goldfish. Flexible liners and fiberglass shells have made pool-building feasible for virtually any do-it-yourselfer. For the experienced mason, a formal pool or wall fountain is another option.

If you prefer not to do the installation yourself, you can hire a landscape professional.

Tub Gardens

If you want to start modestly, small decorative garden pools that are both portable and versatile are widely available in garden supply and statuary

stores. For a slightly larger tub garden, buy at least a 25-gallon container. Or fashion your own from any leakproof vessel, such as a wooden half-barrel. You can always slip the container inside a more handsome—but less seaworthy—barrel or tub.

Before placing a wooden, metal, or unglazed ceramic container in its permanent location, coat the inside with epoxy paint or line it with a flexible liner (see below). A dark-colored coating makes the surface more reflective. A tiny fountain jet, driven by a submersible pump, provides visual interest as well as oxygen for water plants or goldfish.

The Natural Look

In the past, natural-looking pools were made of reinforced concrete; today, do-it-yourselfers may opt for flexible liners or fiberglass shells. It's the border that counts: typically, edges are camouflaged either with lush plantings or with rocks or other masonry materials so the pool looks like a work of nature.

Flexible liners are the big news in garden pools, and you'll find some type of liner in virtually every mail-order garden-pool catalog. Those stout sheets—20 to 30 mils and thicker—are designed especially for garden pools. Though PVC plastic is the

Garden Pool Designs

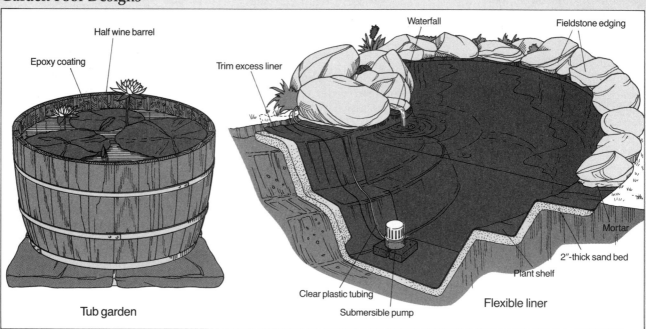

Half wine barrel

Epoxy coating

Trim excess liner

Waterfall

Fieldstone edging

Mortar

2"-thick sand bed

Plant shelf

Clear plastic tubing

Submersible pump

Tub garden

Flexible liner

standard material, it becomes brittle with exposure to the sun's rays; its life expectancy is about 10 years. More UV-resistant—but twice the price—are industrial-grade PVC or butyl-rubber liners. Most liner materials can be cut and solvent-welded to fit odd-shaped water features.

Liner installation is straightforward. First, dig a hole to the contours you wish, adding 2 inches all around for a layer of sand. Level the top of the excavation and add fine, damp sand; smooth with a float or trowel. Drape the liner over the opening, weight the edges, and slowly fill the hole with water while working the liner into shape. Finally, trim all but about 6 inches of excess liner around the edges and finish up with the edging of your choice.

Another option is a fiberglass pool shell—think of it as a spa buried in the ground and filled with plants and fish. A number of shapes and sizes are available, but many are too shallow to house fish. Though they're much more expensive than PVC pools, life expectancy is longer—more than 20 years.

A fiberglass pool shell is easy to install: basically, you shape a hole that follows the shell's outline, lower the unit into place, level it, and backfill with a sand-soil mixture while adding water in 4-inch increments. If you want to hide the lip, over-hang flagstones, fieldstones, or brick an inch or two over the water.

Formal Pools & Wall Fountains

Generally symmetrical in shape and made of masonry, formal pools and fountains can be above ground level or sunken, depending on the site and the desired border effect. A raised pool is more difficult to build, but it provides surfaces for sitting and sunning, as well as for container plants and decorations.

For fast, inexpensive masonry construction, it's hard to beat concrete blocks. Those rugged units make strong cores for formal pools or wall fountains; for a warmer appearance, veneer them with brick, stone, tile, or plaster.

The drawing below shows a typical concrete-block wall fountain. Reinforced and grouted bond-beam blocks cap the walls, substantially increasing the strength. A 4-inch concrete floor completes the structure. For leakproof results, treat the blocks with two coats of a commercial, cement-base waterproofing compound or another liquid membrane before veneering. Or line the inside with a flexible liner; then cap or cover it with more masonry.

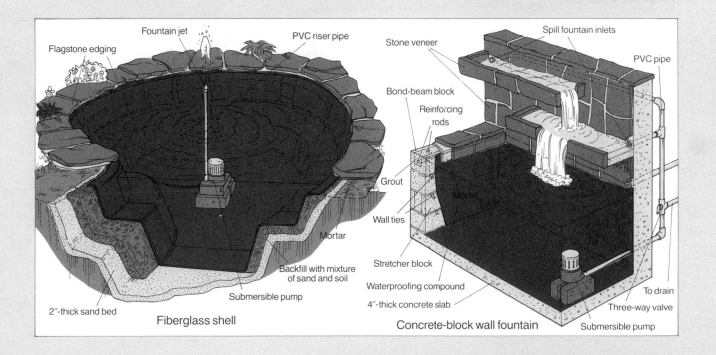

Fiberglass shell

- Fountain jet
- Flagstone edging
- PVC riser pipe
- Mortar
- Backfill with mixture of sand and soil
- Submersible pump
- 2"-thick sand bed

Concrete-block wall fountain

- Stone veneer
- Spill fountain inlets
- PVC pipe
- Bond-beam block
- Reinforcing rods
- Grout
- Mortar
- Wall ties
- Stretcher block
- Waterproofing compound
- 4"-thick concrete slab
- To drain
- Three-way valve
- Submersible pump

Proof-of-Purchase
ISBN 0-376-01399-0 (SB)
ISBN 0-376-09044-8 (SL)

INDEX